C-629　　CAREER EXAMINATION SERIES

This is your
PASSBOOK for...

Public Health Assistant

Test Preparation Study Guide
Questions & Answers

COPYRIGHT NOTICE

This book is SOLELY intended for, is sold ONLY to, and its use is RESTRICTED to individual, bona fide applicants or candidates who qualify by virtue of having seriously filed applications for appropriate license, certificate, professional and/or promotional advancement, higher school matriculation, scholarship, or other legitimate requirements of education and/or governmental authorities.

This book is NOT intended for use, class instruction, tutoring, training, duplication, copying, reprinting, excerption, or adaptation, etc., by:

1) Other publishers
2) Proprietors and/or Instructors of "Coaching" and/or Preparatory Courses
3) Personnel and/or Training Divisions of commercial, industrial, and governmental organizations
4) Schools, colleges, or universities and/or their departments and staffs, including teachers and other personnel
5) Testing Agencies or Bureaus
6) Study groups which seek by the purchase of a single volume to copy and/or duplicate and/or adapt this material for use by the group as a whole without having purchased individual volumes for each of the members of the group
7) Et al.

Such persons would be in violation of appropriate Federal and State statutes.

PROVISION OF LICENSING AGREEMENTS – Recognized educational, commercial, industrial, and governmental institutions and organizations, and others legitimately engaged in educational pursuits, including training, testing, and measurement activities, may address request for a licensing agreement to the copyright owners, who will determine whether, and under what conditions, including fees and charges, the materials in this book may be used them. In other words, a licensing facility exists for the legitimate use of the material in this book on other than an individual basis. However, it is asseverated and affirmed here that the material in this book CANNOT be used without the receipt of the express permission of such a licensing agreement from the Publishers. Inquiries re licensing should be addressed to the company, attention rights and permissions department.

All rights reserved, including the right of reproduction in whole or in part, in any form or by any means, electronic or mechanical, including photocopying, recording, or by any information storage and retrieval system, without permission in writing from the Publisher.

Copyright © 2024 by
National Learning Corporation

212 Michael Drive, Syosset, NY 11791
(516) 921-8888 • www.passbooks.com
E-mail: info@passbooks.com

PUBLISHED IN THE UNITED STATES OF AMERICA

PASSBOOK® SERIES

THE *PASSBOOK® SERIES* has been created to prepare applicants and candidates for the ultimate academic battlefield – the examination room.

At some time in our lives, each and every one of us may be required to take an examination – for validation, matriculation, admission, qualification, registration, certification, or licensure.

Based on the assumption that every applicant or candidate has met the basic formal educational standards, has taken the required number of courses, and read the necessary texts, the *PASSBOOK® SERIES* furnishes the one special preparation which may assure passing with confidence, instead of failing with insecurity. Examination questions – together with answers – are furnished as the basic vehicle for study so that the mysteries of the examination and its compounding difficulties may be eliminated or diminished by a sure method.

This book is meant to help you pass your examination provided that you qualify and are serious in your objective.

The entire field is reviewed through the huge store of content information which is succinctly presented through a provocative and challenging approach – the question-and-answer method.

A climate of success is established by furnishing the correct answers at the end of each test.

You soon learn to recognize types of questions, forms of questions, and patterns of questioning. You may even begin to anticipate expected outcomes.

You perceive that many questions are repeated or adapted so that you can gain acute insights, which may enable you to score many sure points.

You learn how to confront new questions, or types of questions, and to attack them confidently and work out the correct answers.

You note objectives and emphases, and recognize pitfalls and dangers, so that you may make positive educational adjustments.

Moreover, you are kept fully informed in relation to new concepts, methods, practices, and directions in the field.

You discover that you are actually taking the examination all the time: you are preparing for the examination by "taking" an examination, not by reading extraneous and/or supererogatory textbooks.

In short, this PASSBOOK®, used directedly, should be an important factor in helping you to pass your test.

PUBLIC HEALTH ASSISTANT

JOB DESCRIPTION
Under direct supervision, assists medical and/or professional staff in schools and public health clinics by performing clerical and health-related duties; performs related work.

EXAMPLES OF TYPICAL TASKS
Performs vision, hearing and simple urinalysis tests; weighs and measures patients; takes pulse, respiration rates and temperatures; collects specimens; prepares patients for examination and assists professional staff during examination; operates related equipment; may administer simple first aid; interviews clients to obtain identifying and routine medical information; explains testing and clinic procedures to clients; answers routine questions and makes appropriate referrals; makes and receives related telephone calls; comforts patients, reports relevant observations and information to the professional staff; may accompany nurse on home visits; organizes, maintains, retrieves and replaces medical folders, charts and forms; reviews for completeness, and records and transcribes medical information onto appropriate forms, documents, and charts; labels specimens; serves as a receptionist, schedules medical appointments; and contacts patients via telephone or mail regarding appointments; sends, receives and sorts mail, medical records and notices; collects and records statistical data; maintains logs and schedules; requests, arranges and maintains equipment and supplies; does light housekeeping and cleaning of instruments and equipment.

TESTS
The written test may include questions concerning record keeping and office procedures, knowledge of terms and equipment used in clinics or other health centers, judgment, ability to follow directions, sanitation and storing methods, and related matters.

HOW TO TAKE A TEST

I. YOU MUST PASS AN EXAMINATION

A. *WHAT EVERY CANDIDATE SHOULD KNOW*

Examination applicants often ask us for help in preparing for the written test. What can I study in advance? What kinds of questions will be asked? How will the test be given? How will the papers be graded?

As an applicant for a civil service examination, you may be wondering about some of these things. Our purpose here is to suggest effective methods of advance study and to describe civil service examinations.

Your chances for success on this examination can be increased if you know how to prepare. Those "pre-examination jitters" can be reduced if you know what to expect. You can even experience an adventure in good citizenship if you know why civil service exams are given.

B. *WHY ARE CIVIL SERVICE EXAMINATIONS GIVEN?*

Civil service examinations are important to you in two ways. As a citizen, you want public jobs filled by employees who know how to do their work. As a job seeker, you want a fair chance to compete for that job on an equal footing with other candidates. The best-known means of accomplishing this two-fold goal is the competitive examination.

Exams are widely publicized throughout the nation. They may be administered for jobs in federal, state, city, municipal, town or village governments or agencies.

Any citizen may apply, with some limitations, such as the age or residence of applicants. Your experience and education may be reviewed to see whether you meet the requirements for the particular examination. When these requirements exist, they are reasonable and applied consistently to all applicants. Thus, a competitive examination may cause you some uneasiness now, but it is your privilege and safeguard.

C. *HOW ARE CIVIL SERVICE EXAMS DEVELOPED?*

Examinations are carefully written by trained technicians who are specialists in the field known as "psychological measurement," in consultation with recognized authorities in the field of work that the test will cover. These experts recommend the subject matter areas or skills to be tested; only those knowledges or skills important to your success on the job are included. The most reliable books and source materials available are used as references. Together, the experts and technicians judge the difficulty level of the questions.

Test technicians know how to phrase questions so that the problem is clearly stated. Their ethics do not permit "trick" or "catch" questions. Questions may have been tried out on sample groups, or subjected to statistical analysis, to determine their usefulness.

Written tests are often used in combination with performance tests, ratings of training and experience, and oral interviews. All of these measures combine to form the best-known means of finding the right person for the right job.

II. HOW TO PASS THE WRITTEN TEST

A. NATURE OF THE EXAMINATION

To prepare intelligently for civil service examinations, you should know how they differ from school examinations you have taken. In school you were assigned certain definite pages to read or subjects to cover. The examination questions were quite detailed and usually emphasized memory. Civil service exams, on the other hand, try to discover your present ability to perform the duties of a position, plus your potentiality to learn these duties. In other words, a civil service exam attempts to predict how successful you will be. Questions cover such a broad area that they cannot be as minute and detailed as school exam questions.

In the public service similar kinds of work, or positions, are grouped together in one "class." This process is known as *position-classification*. All the positions in a class are paid according to the salary range for that class. One class title covers all of these positions, and they are all tested by the same examination.

B. FOUR BASIC STEPS

1) Study the announcement

How, then, can you know what subjects to study? Our best answer is: "Learn as much as possible about the class of positions for which you've applied." The exam will test the knowledge, skills and abilities needed to do the work.

Your most valuable source of information about the position you want is the official exam announcement. This announcement lists the training and experience qualifications. Check these standards and apply only if you come reasonably close to meeting them.

The brief description of the position in the examination announcement offers some clues to the subjects which will be tested. Think about the job itself. Review the duties in your mind. Can you perform them, or are there some in which you are rusty? Fill in the blank spots in your preparation.

Many jurisdictions preview the written test in the exam announcement by including a section called "Knowledge and Abilities Required," "Scope of the Examination," or some similar heading. Here you will find out specifically what fields will be tested.

2) Review your own background

Once you learn in general what the position is all about, and what you need to know to do the work, ask yourself which subjects you already know fairly well and which need improvement. You may wonder whether to concentrate on improving your strong areas or on building some background in your fields of weakness. When the announcement has specified "some knowledge" or "considerable knowledge," or has used adjectives like "beginning principles of…" or "advanced … methods," you can get a clue as to the number and difficulty of questions to be asked in any given field. More questions, and hence broader coverage, would be included for those subjects which are more important in the work. Now weigh your strengths and weaknesses against the job requirements and prepare accordingly.

3) Determine the level of the position

Another way to tell how intensively you should prepare is to understand the level of the job for which you are applying. Is it the entering level? In other words, is this the position in which beginners in a field of work are hired? Or is it an intermediate or advanced level? Sometimes this is indicated by such words as "Junior" or "Senior" in the class title. Other jurisdictions use Roman numerals to designate the level – Clerk I, Clerk II, for example. The word "Supervisor" sometimes appears in the title. If the level is not indicated by the title, check the description of duties. Will you be working under very close supervision, or will you have responsibility for independent decisions in this work?

4) Choose appropriate study materials

Now that you know the subjects to be examined and the relative amount of each subject to be covered, you can choose suitable study materials. For beginning level jobs, or even advanced ones, if you have a pronounced weakness in some aspect of your training, read a modern, standard textbook in that field. Be sure it is up to date and has general coverage. Such books are normally available at your library, and the librarian will be glad to help you locate one. For entry-level positions, questions of appropriate difficulty are chosen – neither highly advanced questions, nor those too simple. Such questions require careful thought but not advanced training.

If the position for which you are applying is technical or advanced, you will read more advanced, specialized material. If you are already familiar with the basic principles of your field, elementary textbooks would waste your time. Concentrate on advanced textbooks and technical periodicals. Think through the concepts and review difficult problems in your field.

These are all general sources. You can get more ideas on your own initiative, following these leads. For example, training manuals and publications of the government agency which employs workers in your field can be useful, particularly for technical and professional positions. A letter or visit to the government department involved may result in more specific study suggestions, and certainly will provide you with a more definite idea of the exact nature of the position you are seeking.

III. KINDS OF TESTS

Tests are used for purposes other than measuring knowledge and ability to perform specified duties. For some positions, it is equally important to test ability to make adjustments to new situations or to profit from training. In others, basic mental abilities not dependent on information are essential. Questions which test these things may not appear as pertinent to the duties of the position as those which test for knowledge and information. Yet they are often highly important parts of a fair examination. For very general questions, it is almost impossible to help you direct your study efforts. What we can do is to point out some of the more common of these general abilities needed in public service positions and describe some typical questions.

1) General information

Broad, general information has been found useful for predicting job success in some kinds of work. This is tested in a variety of ways, from vocabulary lists to questions about current events. Basic background in some field of work, such as sociology or economics, may be sampled in a group of questions. Often these are principles which have become familiar to most persons through exposure rather than through formal training. It is difficult to advise you how to study for these questions; being alert to the world around you is our best suggestion.

2) Verbal ability

An example of an ability needed in many positions is verbal or language ability. Verbal ability is, in brief, the ability to use and understand words. Vocabulary and grammar tests are typical measures of this ability. Reading comprehension or paragraph interpretation questions are common in many kinds of civil service tests. You are given a paragraph of written material and asked to find its central meaning.

3) Numerical ability

Number skills can be tested by the familiar arithmetic problem, by checking paired lists of numbers to see which are alike and which are different, or by interpreting charts and graphs. In the latter test, a graph may be printed in the test booklet which you are asked to use as the basis for answering questions.

4) Observation

A popular test for law-enforcement positions is the observation test. A picture is shown to you for several minutes, then taken away. Questions about the picture test your ability to observe both details and larger elements.

5) Following directions

In many positions in the public service, the employee must be able to carry out written instructions dependably and accurately. You may be given a chart with several columns, each column listing a variety of information. The questions require you to carry out directions involving the information given in the chart.

6) Skills and aptitudes

Performance tests effectively measure some manual skills and aptitudes. When the skill is one in which you are trained, such as typing or shorthand, you can practice. These tests are often very much like those given in business school or high school courses. For many of the other skills and aptitudes, however, no short-time preparation can be made. Skills and abilities natural to you or that you have developed throughout your lifetime are being tested.

Many of the general questions just described provide all the data needed to answer the questions and ask you to use your reasoning ability to find the answers. Your best preparation for these tests, as well as for tests of facts and ideas, is to be at your physical and mental best. You, no doubt, have your own methods of getting into an exam-taking mood and keeping "in shape." The next section lists some ideas on this subject.

IV. KINDS OF QUESTIONS

Only rarely is the "essay" question, which you answer in narrative form, used in civil service tests. Civil service tests are usually of the short-answer type. Full instructions for answering these questions will be given to you at the examination. But in case this is your first experience with short-answer questions and separate answer sheets, here is what you need to know:

1) Multiple-choice Questions

Most popular of the short-answer questions is the "multiple choice" or "best answer" question. It can be used, for example, to test for factual knowledge, ability to solve problems or judgment in meeting situations found at work.

A multiple-choice question is normally one of three types—
- It can begin with an incomplete statement followed by several possible endings. You are to find the one ending which *best* completes the statement, although some of the others may not be entirely wrong.
- It can also be a complete statement in the form of a question which is answered by choosing one of the statements listed.

- It can be in the form of a problem – again you select the best answer.

Here is an example of a multiple-choice question with a discussion which should give you some clues as to the method for choosing the right answer:

When an employee has a complaint about his assignment, the action which will *best* help him overcome his difficulty is to
   A. discuss his difficulty with his coworkers
   B. take the problem to the head of the organization
   C. take the problem to the person who gave him the assignment
   D. say nothing to anyone about his complaint

In answering this question, you should study each of the choices to find which is best. Consider choice "A" – Certainly an employee may discuss his complaint with fellow employees, but no change or improvement can result, and the complaint remains unresolved. Choice "B" is a poor choice since the head of the organization probably does not know what assignment you have been given, and taking your problem to him is known as "going over the head" of the supervisor. The supervisor, or person who made the assignment, is the person who can clarify it or correct any injustice. Choice "C" is, therefore, correct. To say nothing, as in choice "D," is unwise. Supervisors have and interest in knowing the problems employees are facing, and the employee is seeking a solution to his problem.

2) True/False Questions

The "true/false" or "right/wrong" form of question is sometimes used. Here a complete statement is given. Your job is to decide whether the statement is right or wrong.

SAMPLE: A roaming cell-phone call to a nearby city costs less than a non-roaming call to a distant city.

This statement is wrong, or false, since roaming calls are more expensive.

This is not a complete list of all possible question forms, although most of the others are variations of these common types. You will always get complete directions for answering questions. Be sure you understand *how* to mark your answers – ask questions until you do.

V. RECORDING YOUR ANSWERS

Computer terminals are used more and more today for many different kinds of exams.
For an examination with very few applicants, you may be told to record your answers in the test booklet itself. Separate answer sheets are much more common. If this separate answer sheet is to be scored by machine – and this is often the case – it is highly important that you mark your answers correctly in order to get credit.
An electronic scoring machine is often used in civil service offices because of the speed with which papers can be scored. Machine-scored answer sheets must be marked with a pencil, which will be given to you. This pencil has a high graphite content which responds to the electronic scoring machine. As a matter of fact, stray dots may register as answers, so do not let your pencil rest on the answer sheet while you are pondering the correct answer. Also, if your pencil lead breaks or is otherwise defective, ask for another.

Since the answer sheet will be dropped in a slot in the scoring machine, be careful not to bend the corners or get the paper crumpled.

The answer sheet normally has five vertical columns of numbers, with 30 numbers to a column. These numbers correspond to the question numbers in your test booklet. After each number, going across the page are four or five pairs of dotted lines. These short dotted lines have small letters or numbers above them. The first two pairs may also have a "T" or "F" above the letters. This indicates that the first two pairs only are to be used if the questions are of the true-false type. If the questions are multiple choice, disregard the "T" and "F" and pay attention only to the small letters or numbers.

Answer your questions in the manner of the sample that follows:

32. The largest city in the United States is
    A. Washington, D.C.
    B. New York City
    C. Chicago
    D. Detroit
    E. San Francisco

1) Choose the answer you think is best. (New York City is the largest, so "B" is correct.)
2) Find the row of dotted lines numbered the same as the question you are answering. (Find row number 32)
3) Find the pair of dotted lines corresponding to the answer. (Find the pair of lines under the mark "B.")
4) Make a solid black mark between the dotted lines.

VI. BEFORE THE TEST

Common sense will help you find procedures to follow to get ready for an examination. Too many of us, however, overlook these sensible measures. Indeed, nervousness and fatigue have been found to be the most serious reasons why applicants fail to do their best on civil service tests. Here is a list of reminders:

- Begin your preparation early – Don't wait until the last minute to go scurrying around for books and materials or to find out what the position is all about.
- Prepare continuously – An hour a night for a week is better than an all-night cram session. This has been definitely established. What is more, a night a week for a month will return better dividends than crowding your study into a shorter period of time.
- Locate the place of the exam – You have been sent a notice telling you when and where to report for the examination. If the location is in a different town or otherwise unfamiliar to you, it would be well to inquire the best route and learn something about the building.
- Relax the night before the test – Allow your mind to rest. Do not study at all that night. Plan some mild recreation or diversion; then go to bed early and get a good night's sleep.
- Get up early enough to make a leisurely trip to the place for the test – This way unforeseen events, traffic snarls, unfamiliar buildings, etc. will not upset you.
- Dress comfortably – A written test is not a fashion show. You will be known by number and not by name, so wear something comfortable.

- Leave excess paraphernalia at home – Shopping bags and odd bundles will get in your way. You need bring only the items mentioned in the official notice you received; usually everything you need is provided. Do not bring reference books to the exam. They will only confuse those last minutes and be taken away from you when in the test room.
- Arrive somewhat ahead of time – If because of transportation schedules you must get there very early, bring a newspaper or magazine to take your mind off yourself while waiting.
- Locate the examination room – When you have found the proper room, you will be directed to the seat or part of the room where you will sit. Sometimes you are given a sheet of instructions to read while you are waiting. Do not fill out any forms until you are told to do so; just read them and be prepared.
- Relax and prepare to listen to the instructions
- If you have any physical problem that may keep you from doing your best, be sure to tell the test administrator. If you are sick or in poor health, you really cannot do your best on the exam. You can come back and take the test some other time.

VII. AT THE TEST

The day of the test is here and you have the test booklet in your hand. The temptation to get going is very strong. Caution! There is more to success than knowing the right answers. You must know how to identify your papers and understand variations in the type of short-answer question used in this particular examination. Follow these suggestions for maximum results from your efforts:

1) Cooperate with the monitor

The test administrator has a duty to create a situation in which you can be as much at ease as possible. He will give instructions, tell you when to begin, check to see that you are marking your answer sheet correctly, and so on. He is not there to guard you, although he will see that your competitors do not take unfair advantage. He wants to help you do your best.

2) Listen to all instructions

Don't jump the gun! Wait until you understand all directions. In most civil service tests you get more time than you need to answer the questions. So don't be in a hurry. Read each word of instructions until you clearly understand the meaning. Study the examples, listen to all announcements and follow directions. Ask questions if you do not understand what to do.

3) Identify your papers

Civil service exams are usually identified by number only. You will be assigned a number; you must not put your name on your test papers. Be sure to copy your number correctly. Since more than one exam may be given, copy your exact examination title.

4) Plan your time

Unless you are told that a test is a "speed" or "rate of work" test, speed itself is usually not important. Time enough to answer all the questions will be provided, but this does not mean that you have all day. An overall time limit has been set. Divide the total time (in minutes) by the number of questions to determine the approximate time you have for each question.

5) Do not linger over difficult questions

If you come across a difficult question, mark it with a paper clip (useful to have along) and come back to it when you have been through the booklet. One caution if you do this – be sure to skip a number on your answer sheet as well. Check often to be sure that you have not lost your place and that you are marking in the row numbered the same as the question you are answering.

6) Read the questions

Be sure you know what the question asks! Many capable people are unsuccessful because they failed to *read* the questions correctly.

7) Answer all questions

Unless you have been instructed that a penalty will be deducted for incorrect answers, it is better to guess than to omit a question.

8) Speed tests

It is often better NOT to guess on speed tests. It has been found that on timed tests people are tempted to spend the last few seconds before time is called in marking answers at random – without even reading them – in the hope of picking up a few extra points. To discourage this practice, the instructions may warn you that your score will be "corrected" for guessing. That is, a penalty will be applied. The incorrect answers will be deducted from the correct ones, or some other penalty formula will be used.

9) Review your answers

If you finish before time is called, go back to the questions you guessed or omitted to give them further thought. Review other answers if you have time.

10) Return your test materials

If you are ready to leave before others have finished or time is called, take ALL your materials to the monitor and leave quietly. Never take any test material with you. The monitor can discover whose papers are not complete, and taking a test booklet may be grounds for disqualification.

VIII. EXAMINATION TECHNIQUES

1) Read the general instructions carefully. These are usually printed on the first page of the exam booklet. As a rule, these instructions refer to the timing of the examination; the fact that you should not start work until the signal and must stop work at a signal, etc. If there are any *special* instructions, such as a choice of questions to be answered, make sure that you note this instruction carefully.

2) When you are ready to start work on the examination, that is as soon as the signal has been given, read the instructions to each question booklet, underline any key words or phrases, such as *least, best, outline, describe* and the like. In this way you will tend to answer as requested rather than discover on reviewing your paper that you *listed without describing*, that you selected the *worst* choice rather than the *best* choice, etc.

3) If the examination is of the objective or multiple-choice type – that is, each question will also give a series of possible answers: A, B, C or D, and you are called upon to select the best answer and write the letter next to that answer on your answer paper – it is advisable to start answering each question in turn. There may be anywhere from 50 to 100 such questions in the three or four hours allotted and you can see how much time would be taken if you read through all the questions before beginning to answer any. Furthermore, if you come across a question or group of questions which you know would be difficult to answer, it would undoubtedly affect your handling of all the other questions.

4) If the examination is of the essay type and contains but a few questions, it is a moot point as to whether you should read all the questions before starting to answer any one. Of course, if you are given a choice – say five out of seven and the like – then it is essential to read all the questions so you can eliminate the two that are most difficult. If, however, you are asked to answer all the questions, there may be danger in trying to answer the easiest one first because you may find that you will spend too much time on it. The best technique is to answer the first question, then proceed to the second, etc.

5) Time your answers. Before the exam begins, write down the time it started, then add the time allowed for the examination and write down the time it must be completed, then divide the time available somewhat as follows:
    - If 3-1/2 hours are allowed, that would be 210 minutes. If you have 80 objective-type questions, that would be an average of 2-1/2 minutes per question. Allow yourself no more than 2 minutes per question, or a total of 160 minutes, which will permit about 50 minutes to review.
    - If for the time allotment of 210 minutes there are 7 essay questions to answer, that would average about 30 minutes a question. Give yourself only 25 minutes per question so that you have about 35 minutes to review.

6) The most important instruction is to *read each question* and make sure you know what is wanted. The second most important instruction is to *time yourself properly* so that you answer every question. The third most important instruction is to *answer every question*. Guess if you have to but include something for each question. Remember that you will receive no credit for a blank and will probably receive some credit if you write something in answer to an essay question. If you guess a letter – say "B" for a multiple-choice question – you may have guessed right. If you leave a blank as an answer to a multiple-choice question, the examiners may respect your feelings but it will not add a point to your score. Some exams may penalize you for wrong answers, so in such cases *only*, you may not want to guess unless you have some basis for your answer.

7) Suggestions
    a. Objective-type questions
        1. Examine the question booklet for proper sequence of pages and questions
        2. Read all instructions carefully
        3. Skip any question which seems too difficult; return to it after all other questions have been answered
        4. Apportion your time properly; do not spend too much time on any single question or group of questions

5. Note and underline key words – *all, most, fewest, least, best, worst, same, opposite*, etc.
6. Pay particular attention to negatives
7. Note unusual option, e.g., unduly long, short, complex, different or similar in content to the body of the question
8. Observe the use of "hedging" words – *probably, may, most likely*, etc.
9. Make sure that your answer is put next to the same number as the question
10. Do not second-guess unless you have good reason to believe the second answer is definitely more correct
11. Cross out original answer if you decide another answer is more accurate; do not erase until you are ready to hand your paper in
12. Answer all questions; guess unless instructed otherwise
13. Leave time for review

  b. Essay questions
   1. Read each question carefully
   2. Determine exactly what is wanted. Underline key words or phrases.
   3. Decide on outline or paragraph answer
   4. Include many different points and elements unless asked to develop any one or two points or elements
   5. Show impartiality by giving pros and cons unless directed to select one side only
   6. Make and write down any assumptions you find necessary to answer the questions
   7. Watch your English, grammar, punctuation and choice of words
   8. Time your answers; don't crowd material

8) Answering the essay question

Most essay questions can be answered by framing the specific response around several key words or ideas. Here are a few such key words or ideas:

M's: manpower, materials, methods, money, management
P's: purpose, program, policy, plan, procedure, practice, problems, pitfalls, personnel, public relations
  a. Six basic steps in handling problems:
   1. Preliminary plan and background development
   2. Collect information, data and facts
   3. Analyze and interpret information, data and facts
   4. Analyze and develop solutions as well as make recommendations
   5. Prepare report and sell recommendations
   6. Install recommendations and follow up effectiveness

  b. Pitfalls to avoid
   1. *Taking things for granted* – A statement of the situation does not necessarily imply that each of the elements is necessarily true; for example, a complaint may be invalid and biased so that all that can be taken for granted is that a complaint has been registered

2. *Considering only one side of a situation* – Wherever possible, indicate several alternatives and then point out the reasons you selected the best one
3. *Failing to indicate follow up* – Whenever your answer indicates action on your part, make certain that you will take proper follow-up action to see how successful your recommendations, procedures or actions turn out to be
4. *Taking too long in answering any single question* – Remember to time your answers properly

IX. AFTER THE TEST

Scoring procedures differ in detail among civil service jurisdictions although the general principles are the same. Whether the papers are hand-scored or graded by machine we have described, they are nearly always graded by number. That is, the person who marks the paper knows only the number – never the name – of the applicant. Not until all the papers have been graded will they be matched with names. If other tests, such as training and experience or oral interview ratings have been given, scores will be combined. Different parts of the examination usually have different weights. For example, the written test might count 60 percent of the final grade, and a rating of training and experience 40 percent. In many jurisdictions, veterans will have a certain number of points added to their grades.

After the final grade has been determined, the names are placed in grade order and an eligible list is established. There are various methods for resolving ties between those who get the same final grade – probably the most common is to place first the name of the person whose application was received first. Job offers are made from the eligible list in the order the names appear on it. You will be notified of your grade and your rank as soon as all these computations have been made. This will be done as rapidly as possible.

People who are found to meet the requirements in the announcement are called "eligibles." Their names are put on a list of eligible candidates. An eligible's chances of getting a job depend on how high he stands on this list and how fast agencies are filling jobs from the list.

When a job is to be filled from a list of eligibles, the agency asks for the names of people on the list of eligibles for that job. When the civil service commission receives this request, it sends to the agency the names of the three people highest on this list. Or, if the job to be filled has specialized requirements, the office sends the agency the names of the top three persons who meet these requirements from the general list.

The appointing officer makes a choice from among the three people whose names were sent to him. If the selected person accepts the appointment, the names of the others are put back on the list to be considered for future openings.

That is the rule in hiring from all kinds of eligible lists, whether they are for typist, carpenter, chemist, or something else. For every vacancy, the appointing officer has his choice of any one of the top three eligibles on the list. This explains why the person whose name is on top of the list sometimes does not get an appointment when some of the persons lower on the list do. If the appointing officer chooses the second or third eligible, the No. 1 eligible does not get a job at once, but stays on the list until he is appointed or the list is terminated.

X. HOW TO PASS THE INTERVIEW TEST

The examination for which you applied requires an oral interview test. You have already taken the written test and you are now being called for the interview test – the final part of the formal examination.

You may think that it is not possible to prepare for an interview test and that there are no procedures to follow during an interview. Our purpose is to point out some things you can do in advance that will help you and some good rules to follow and pitfalls to avoid while you are being interviewed.

What is an interview supposed to test?

The written examination is designed to test the technical knowledge and competence of the candidate; the oral is designed to evaluate intangible qualities, not readily measured otherwise, and to establish a list showing the relative fitness of each candidate – as measured against his competitors – for the position sought. Scoring is not on the basis of "right" and "wrong," but on a sliding scale of values ranging from "not passable" to "outstanding." As a matter of fact, it is possible to achieve a relatively low score without a single "incorrect" answer because of evident weakness in the qualities being measured.

Occasionally, an examination may consist entirely of an oral test – either an individual or a group oral. In such cases, information is sought concerning the technical knowledges and abilities of the candidate, since there has been no written examination for this purpose. More commonly, however, an oral test is used to supplement a written examination.

Who conducts interviews?

The composition of oral boards varies among different jurisdictions. In nearly all, a representative of the personnel department serves as chairman. One of the members of the board may be a representative of the department in which the candidate would work. In some cases, "outside experts" are used, and, frequently, a businessman or some other representative of the general public is asked to serve. Labor and management or other special groups may be represented. The aim is to secure the services of experts in the appropriate field.

However the board is composed, it is a good idea (and not at all improper or unethical) to ascertain in advance of the interview who the members are and what groups they represent. When you are introduced to them, you will have some idea of their backgrounds and interests, and at least you will not stutter and stammer over their names.

What should be done before the interview?

While knowledge about the board members is useful and takes some of the surprise element out of the interview, there is other preparation which is more substantive. It *is* possible to prepare for an oral interview – in several ways:

1) Keep a copy of your application and review it carefully before the interview

This may be the only document before the oral board, and the starting point of the interview. Know what education and experience you have listed there, and the sequence and dates of all of it. Sometimes the board will ask you to review the highlights of your experience for them; you should not have to hem and haw doing it.

2) Study the class specification and the examination announcement

Usually, the oral board has one or both of these to guide them. The qualities, characteristics or knowledges required by the position sought are stated in these documents. They offer valuable clues as to the nature of the oral interview. For example, if the job involves supervisory responsibilities, the announcement will usually indicate that knowledge of modern supervisory methods and the qualifications of the candidate as a supervisor will be tested. If so, you can expect such questions, frequently in the form of a hypothetical situation which you are expected to solve. NEVER go into an oral without knowledge of the duties and responsibilities of the job you seek.

3) Think through each qualification required

Try to visualize the kind of questions you would ask if you were a board member. How well could you answer them? Try especially to appraise your own knowledge and background in each area, *measured against the job sought*, and identify any areas in which you are weak. Be critical and realistic – do not flatter yourself.

4) Do some general reading in areas in which you feel you may be weak

For example, if the job involves supervision and your past experience has NOT, some general reading in supervisory methods and practices, particularly in the field of human relations, might be useful. Do NOT study agency procedures or detailed manuals. The oral board will be testing your understanding and capacity, not your memory.

5) Get a good night's sleep and watch your general health and mental attitude

You will want a clear head at the interview. Take care of a cold or any other minor ailment, and of course, no hangovers.

What should be done on the day of the interview?

Now comes the day of the interview itself. Give yourself plenty of time to get there. Plan to arrive somewhat ahead of the scheduled time, particularly if your appointment is in the fore part of the day. If a previous candidate fails to appear, the board might be ready for you a bit early. By early afternoon an oral board is almost invariably behind schedule if there are many candidates, and you may have to wait. Take along a book or magazine to read, or your application to review, but leave any extraneous material in the waiting room when you go in for your interview. In any event, relax and compose yourself.

The matter of dress is important. The board is forming impressions about you – from your experience, your manners, your attitude, and your appearance. Give your personal appearance careful attention. Dress your best, but not your flashiest. Choose conservative, appropriate clothing, and be sure it is immaculate. This is a business interview, and your appearance should indicate that you regard it as such. Besides, being well groomed and properly dressed will help boost your confidence.

Sooner or later, someone will call your name and escort you into the interview room. *This is it.* From here on you are on your own. It is too late for any more preparation. But remember, you asked for this opportunity to prove your fitness, and you are here because your request was granted.

What happens when you go in?

The usual sequence of events will be as follows: The clerk (who is often the board stenographer) will introduce you to the chairman of the oral board, who will introduce you to the other members of the board. Acknowledge the introductions before you sit down. Do not be surprised if you find a microphone facing you or a stenotypist sitting by. Oral interviews are usually recorded in the event of an appeal or other review.

Usually the chairman of the board will open the interview by reviewing the highlights of your education and work experience from your application – primarily for the benefit of the other members of the board, as well as to get the material into the record. Do not interrupt or comment unless there is an error or significant misinterpretation; if that is the case, do not hesitate. But do not quibble about insignificant matters. Also, he will usually ask you some question about your education, experience or your present job – partly to get you to start talking and to establish the interviewing "rapport." He may start the actual questioning, or turn it over to one of the other members. Frequently, each member undertakes the questioning on a particular area, one in which he is perhaps most competent, so you can expect each member to participate in the examination. Because time is limited, you may also expect some rather abrupt switches in the direction the questioning takes, so do not be upset by it. Normally, a board member will not pursue a single line of questioning unless he discovers a particular strength or weakness.

After each member has participated, the chairman will usually ask whether any member has any further questions, then will ask you if you have anything you wish to add. Unless you are expecting this question, it may floor you. Worse, it may start you off on an extended, extemporaneous speech. The board is not usually seeking more information. The question is principally to offer you a last opportunity to present further qualifications or to indicate that you have nothing to add. So, if you feel that a significant qualification or characteristic has been overlooked, it is proper to point it out in a sentence or so. Do not compliment the board on the thoroughness of their examination – they have been sketchy, and you know it. If you wish, merely say, "No thank you, I have nothing further to add." This is a point where you can "talk yourself out" of a good impression or fail to present an important bit of information. Remember, *you close the interview yourself.*

The chairman will then say, "That is all, Mr. _____, thank you." Do not be startled; the interview is over, and quicker than you think. Thank him, gather your belongings and take your leave. Save your sigh of relief for the other side of the door.

How to put your best foot forward

Throughout this entire process, you may feel that the board individually and collectively is trying to pierce your defenses, seek out your hidden weaknesses and embarrass and confuse you. Actually, this is not true. They are obliged to make an appraisal of your qualifications for the job you are seeking, and they want to see you in your best light. Remember, they must interview all candidates and a non-cooperative candidate may become a failure in spite of their best efforts to bring out his qualifications. Here are 15 suggestions that will help you:

1) Be natural – Keep your attitude confident, not cocky

If you are not confident that you can do the job, do not expect the board to be. Do not apologize for your weaknesses, try to bring out your strong points. The board is interested in a positive, not negative, presentation. Cockiness will antagonize any board member and make him wonder if you are covering up a weakness by a false show of strength.

2) Get comfortable, but don't lounge or sprawl

Sit erectly but not stiffly. A careless posture may lead the board to conclude that you are careless in other things, or at least that you are not impressed by the importance of the occasion. Either conclusion is natural, even if incorrect. Do not fuss with your clothing, a pencil or an ashtray. Your hands may occasionally be useful to emphasize a point; do not let them become a point of distraction.

3) Do not wisecrack or make small talk

This is a serious situation, and your attitude should show that you consider it as such. Further, the time of the board is limited – they do not want to waste it, and neither should you.

4) Do not exaggerate your experience or abilities

In the first place, from information in the application or other interviews and sources, the board may know more about you than you think. Secondly, you probably will not get away with it. An experienced board is rather adept at spotting such a situation, so do not take the chance.

5) If you know a board member, do not make a point of it, yet do not hide it

Certainly you are not fooling him, and probably not the other members of the board. Do not try to take advantage of your acquaintanceship – it will probably do you little good.

6) Do not dominate the interview

Let the board do that. They will give you the clues – do not assume that you have to do all the talking. Realize that the board has a number of questions to ask you, and do not try to take up all the interview time by showing off your extensive knowledge of the answer to the first one.

7) Be attentive

You only have 20 minutes or so, and you should keep your attention at its sharpest throughout. When a member is addressing a problem or question to you, give him your undivided attention. Address your reply principally to him, but do not exclude the other board members.

8) Do not interrupt

A board member may be stating a problem for you to analyze. He will ask you a question when the time comes. Let him state the problem, and wait for the question.

9) Make sure you understand the question

Do not try to answer until you are sure what the question is. If it is not clear, restate it in your own words or ask the board member to clarify it for you. However, do not haggle about minor elements.

10) Reply promptly but not hastily

A common entry on oral board rating sheets is "candidate responded readily," or "candidate hesitated in replies." Respond as promptly and quickly as you can, but do not jump to a hasty, ill-considered answer.

11) Do not be peremptory in your answers

A brief answer is proper – but do not fire your answer back. That is a losing game from your point of view. The board member can probably ask questions much faster than you can answer them.

12) Do not try to create the answer you think the board member wants

He is interested in what kind of mind you have and how it works – not in playing games. Furthermore, he can usually spot this practice and will actually grade you down on it.

13) Do not switch sides in your reply merely to agree with a board member

Frequently, a member will take a contrary position merely to draw you out and to see if you are willing and able to defend your point of view. Do not start a debate, yet do not surrender a good position. If a position is worth taking, it is worth defending.

14) Do not be afraid to admit an error in judgment if you are shown to be wrong

The board knows that you are forced to reply without any opportunity for careful consideration. Your answer may be demonstrably wrong. If so, admit it and get on with the interview.

15) Do not dwell at length on your present job

The opening question may relate to your present assignment. Answer the question but do not go into an extended discussion. You are being examined for a *new* job, not your present one. As a matter of fact, try to phrase ALL your answers in terms of the job for which you are being examined.

Basis of Rating

Probably you will forget most of these "do's" and "don'ts" when you walk into the oral interview room. Even remembering them all will not ensure you a passing grade. Perhaps you did not have the qualifications in the first place. But remembering them will help you to put your best foot forward, without treading on the toes of the board members.

Rumor and popular opinion to the contrary notwithstanding, an oral board wants you to make the best appearance possible. They know you are under pressure – but they also want to see how you respond to it as a guide to what your reaction would be under the pressures of the job you seek. They will be influenced by the degree of poise you display, the personal traits you show and the manner in which you respond.

ABOUT THIS BOOK

This book contains tests divided into Examination Sections. Go through each test, answering every question in the margin. We have also attached a sample answer sheet at the back of the book that can be removed and used. At the end of each test look at the answer key and check your answers. On the ones you got wrong, look at the right answer choice and learn. Do not fill in the answers first. Do not memorize the questions and answers, but understand the answer and principles involved. On your test, the questions will likely be different from the samples. Questions are changed and new ones added. If you understand these past questions you should have success with any changes that arise. Tests may consist of several types of questions. We have additional books on each subject should more study be advisable or necessary for you. Finally, the more you study, the better prepared you will be. This book is intended to be the last thing you study before you walk into the examination room. Prior study of relevant texts is also recommended. NLC publishes some of these in our Fundamental Series. Knowledge and good sense are important factors in passing your exam. Good luck also helps. So now study this Passbook, absorb the material contained within and take that knowledge into the examination. Then do your best to pass that exam.

EXAMINATION SECTION

EXAMINATION SECTION
TEST 1

DIRECTIONS: Each question or incomplete statement is followed by several suggested answers or completions. Select the one that BEST answers the question or completes the statement. *PRINT THE LETTER OF THE CORRECT ANSWER IN THE SPACE AT THE RIGHT.*

1. Of the following, the one which is NOT considered to be a duty of the assistant is to

    A. interview the patients
    B. administer local anaesthesia to a patient
    C. take the temperature of patients
    D. aid the patient in preparing for a medical examination

2. Assume that a patient appears at your clinic at 11:00 on a busy day while you are on duty in the reception room. He says that he missed his 9:00 appointment and that he must return to work within an hour.
The one of the following which is the MOST acceptable course of action for you to take FIRST is to

    A. ask the others who are waiting if they will allow this patient to precede them
    B. immediately schedule another appointment for the patient for the same day in the following week
    C. take the patient to the examining room to see the doctor immediately
    D. explain to the patient that others are waiting and ask him to wait his turn

3. As an assistant, you will be required to follow certain instructions of the doctor or nurse in the administration of the clinic. Suppose that you have been given some instructions by the doctor which you do not completely understand.
The one of the following which is the MOST advisable course of conduct for you to follow is to

    A. carry out the instructions to the best of your ability
    B. ask another employee in the clinic to interpret the order to you
    C. ask the doctor to repeat the instructions or to clarify them
    D. disregard the instructions and wait until the doctor speaks to you again

4. As the assistant assigned to a district health center, you are required to interview new patients briefly to determine which clinics they are to go to. There are a number of patients waiting to talk to you. The person whom you are interviewing is Italian and speaks English so poorly that it is almost impossible for you to understand her. She is also very upset and excited. You know that one of the clerks in the eye clinic speaks Italian.
For you to call that clerk and ask him to act as interpreter is

    A. *inadvisable;* the information you must get is confidential and should not be known to the clerk
    B. *advisable* ; the person you are interviewing will be more comfortable in her own language and the interview will, therefore, be completed more quickly
    C. *inadvisable;* the clerk you wish to call may not want to act as interpreter
    D. *advisable;* you will not be responsible for any misunderstanding in this situation if someone else did the interviewing

5. You are assigned to a chest clinic. One Saturday morning, you are alone in the clinic. The doctor has telephoned that he will be delayed and the nurse has not yet reported. One of the regular clinic patients begins coughing while she is talking to you and has a severe hemorrhage.
   The BEST procedure for you to follow in this situation is to

   A. give the patient a stimulant and apply a cold compress to the back of the neck
   B. look in the other clinics to see if there is anyone else on duty
   C. do nothing until the doctor comes in
   D. call the police for an ambulance

6. Suppose that you are assigned to interviewing incoming patients for certain routine information in a busy dental clinic. You learn that some patients go to the eye clinic after you have interviewed them where another assistant interviews them for the same information. The two sets of information are to be kept in permanent card files, in two separate clinic offices.
   Of the following suggestions which you might make to your supervisor, the one which would prove to be MOST helpful in simplifying this procedure would be for you to

   A. continue to record the information separately so that you can check your records with those of the other assistant for possible errors
   B. send the patient to the other clinic first since they may need more information than you do
   C. fill out two record cards and forward one card to the other clinic
   D. send your record card to the other clinic with the patient after he has been examined by the doctor

7. Suppose that a visitor calls at your clinic and requests information concerning the medical history of a patient. Of the following, the MOST acceptable action for you to take is to

   A. ask him why he wants the information so that you may determine if there is sufficient reason for you to give him the information
   B. give him the information readily as this will foster favorable public relations
   C. refer him to the doctor who examined the patient as he is in a better position to know the patient's medical history
   D. explain that you cannot give out such information as it is strictly confidential and suggest that he write to the department for the information

8. To equip a corner of the outer office of a health center with toys is

   A. *advisable;* the children will be occupied while waiting and, therefore, will be more manageable during the doctor's examination and treatment
   B. *inadvisable;* the child may become too absorbed in play to submit to examination
   C. *advisable;* the children will be so absorbed in play that they will not be aware of whatever discomfort is caused by treatment
   D. *inadvisable;* playing may overstimulate the child and thus cause inaccurate results in the examination

9. While working in a clinic, you discover some obvious inconsistencies in the filing system as a whole. You also have in mind a corrective measure which you would like to see put into practice.
The one of the following which is the MOST acceptable procedure for you to follow is to

   A. try out your new system for a few days to determine its success before discussing it with your supervisor
   B. explain the probable advantages of your proposed plan to your supervisor and secure his approval before making any changes
   C. continue working under the old procedure until the inconsistencies become apparent to the rest of the staff
   D. collect sufficient evidence to prove the obvious inconsistencies in the present filing system in order to convince your supervisor that the system is unsatisfactory

10. Assume that you are in charge of the patients' files in the health center to which you are assigned. The record cards of the individual patients are filed alphabetically according to the name of the patient. You want to make it easier to pick out the cards of those patients who are under treatment for any one of five indicated diseases. Of the following, the procedure which would be MOST helpful for this purpose would be to

    A. insert the card of each patient having one of the five diseases into a special folder
    B. use a different size card for each of the five diseases
    C. use a different color card for each of the five diseases
    D. underline the name of the disease on each card in the file

11. Assume that you are assigned to the chest clinic where you are responsible for the patients' x-ray records. The doctor in charge tells you that in an old group of about 250 disarranged pictures, he thinks there may be several instances in which more than one record exists for the same patient. He asks you to pick out any such records and give them to him.
Of the following, the BEST procedure for you to follow FIRST is to

    A. look at each record in turn, number it, and make a list of the numbers and corresponding names
    B. go through the records quickly and pick out those names which you remember
    C. arrange the records in alphabetical order according to the names of the patients
    D. list the names of all the patients whose records appear in the group

12. As an assistant, one of your principal duties is the proper maintenance of the supply cabinet of the clinic to which you are assigned. Upon inspecting the cabinet, you find several large containers with identical labels. However, these contain pills of different color and shapes. Of the following, the MOST acceptable course of conduct for you to follow is to

    A. attempt to sort the pills and relabel them on the basis of your own knowledge
    B. throw all of the pills away to make certain they will not be misused
    C. inform the doctor that you have relabeled the containers after sorting the pills
    D. inform the doctor of the situation so that he may decide what is to be done

13. Assume that a patient arrives at the clinic and demands an immediate appointment at a time when the doctor is busy.
Of the following, the action which is MOST acceptable for you to take is to

   A. give the patient a sedative to quiet his nerves and guide him to an unoccupied examination room to rest
   B. explain to the patient that the doctor is busy and ask him to be seated in the waiting room
   C. ask the doctor to examine the patient immediately
   D. talk to the patient until the doctor is ready

14. One of your duties in the clinic is the weighing and measurement of adult patients.
Of the following, the procedure which is NOT necessary to secure accurate weighing of patients is

   A. daily testing and adjustment of the scale for accurate balance
   B. instructing the patient to stand firmly in the center of the scale
   C. noting what type of clothing the patient is wearing
   D. placing a clean paper towel on the scale before each patient is weighed

15. Suppose that a patient in the clinic is in immediate need of first aid for shock.
The MOST important thing to do first when both the doctor and nurse are absent is to

   A. make the patient as comfortable as possible and administer a sedative
   B. keep the patient on his feet and moving about in order to activate blood circulation throughout the body
   C. keep the patient as warm as possible
   D. try to locate the doctor before attempting any independent action

16. A patient reports for her scheduled appointment in the pre-natal clinic and tells you, while she is waiting to be examined, that she has a very severe pain in her back. Of the following, the MOST acceptable action for you to take is to

   A. express sympathy and tell her that you yourself once had a severe backache for which it was difficult to get any relief
   B. tell her politely not to take up your time with her ailments as you have other things to do
   C. recommend a liniment which you have used and found to be very helpful in such cases
   D. suggest that she speak to the doctor about it when he examines her

17. A *ticketer system* in a health center may be used as a

   A. follow-up procedure for the recall of patients
   B. method of charting blood pressure recordings at each visit
   C. standard procedure for recording information to be included in memoranda to the doctors
   D. series of tests of nervous reactions

18. When papers are filed according to the date of their receipt, they are said to be filed

   A. numerically   B. geographically
   C. chronologically   D. alphabetically

19. The one of the following which is the MOST important requirement of a good filing system is that 19.____

   A. the expense of installation and operation be low
   B. papers be found easily when needed
   C. the system be capable of any amount of expansion which may be necessary in the future
   D. the filing system have a cross-reference index

Questions 20-24.

DIRECTIONS: Questions 20 through 24 consist of a group of names which are to be arranged in alphabetical order for filing.

20. Of the following, the name which should be filed FIRST is 20.____

   A. Joseph J. Meadeen   B. Gerard L. Meader
   C. John F. Madcar   D. Philip F. Malder

21. Of the following, the name which should be filed LAST is 21.____

   A. Stephen Fischer   B. Benjamin Fitchmann
   C. Thomas Fishman   D. Augustus S. Fisher

22. The name which should be filed SECOND is 22.____

   A. Yeatman, Frances   B. Yeaton, C.S.
   C. Yeatman, R.M.   D. Yeats, John

23. The name which should be filed THIRD is 23.____

   A. Hauser, Ann   B. Hauptmann, Jane
   C. Hauster, Mary   D. Hauprich, Julia

24. The name which should be filed SECOND is 24.____

   A. Flora McDougall   B. Fred E. MacDowell
   C. Juanita Mendez   D. James A. Madden

25. The *initial* contact is of great importance in setting a pattern for future relations. 25.____
    The word *initial,* as used in this sentence, means MOST NEARLY

   A. first   B. written   C. direct   D. hidden

26. The doctor prescribed a diet which was *adequate* for the patient's needs. 26.____
    The word *adequate,* as used in this sentence, means MOST NEARLY

   A. insufficient   B. unusual
   C. required   D. enough

27. The child was reported to be suffering from a vitamin *deficiency.* 27.____
    The word *deficiency,* as used in this sentence, means MOST NEARLY

   A. surplus   B. infection   C. shortage   D. injury

28. In obtaining medical case data, a medical record librarian should discourage the patient from giving *irrelevant* information.
    The word *irrelevant*, as used in this sentence means MOST NEARLY

    A. too detailed
    B. pertaining to relatives
    C. insufficient
    D. inappropriate

29. The doctor requested that a *tentative* appointment be made for the patient.
    The word *tentative*, as used in this sentence, means MOST NEARLY

    A. definite
    B. subject to change
    C. later
    D. of short duration

30. The black plague resulted in an usually high *mortality rate* in the population of Europe.
    The term *mortality rate*, as used in this sentence, means MOST NEARLY

    A. future immunity of the people
    B. death rate
    C. general weakening of the health of the people
    D. sickness rate

31. The public health assistant was asked to file a number of *identical* reports on the case.
    The word *identical*, as used in this sentence, means MOST NEARLY

    A. accurate   B. detailed   C. same   D. different

32. The nurse assisted in the *biopsy* of the patient.
    The word *biopsy*, as used in this sentence, means MOST NEARLY

    A. autopsy
    B. excision and diagnostic study of tissue
    C. biography and health history
    D. administering of anesthesia

33. The assistant noted that the swelling on the patient's face had *subsided*.
    The word *subsided*, as used in this sentence, means MOST NEARLY

    A. become aggravated
    B. increased
    C. vanished
    D. abated

34. The patient was given food *intravenously*.
    The word *intravenously*, as used in this sentence, means MOST NEARLY

    A. orally
    B. against his will
    C. through the veins
    D. without condiment

Questions 35-40.

DIRECTIONS: Questions 35 through 40 are to be answered on the basis of the chart below.

SEMI-ANNUAL REPORT OF EXPENDITURES FOR SUPPLIES AND EQUIPMENT
Health Center X - January to June

MONTH	BABY	CHEST	DENTAL	PRE-NATAL	X-RAY	TOTAL
January $	456.32	$204.28	$723.22	$436.29	$153.25	$1,973.36
February	425.59	225.27	743.33	452.51	174.42	2,021.12
March	631.93	226.35	716.29	429.33	173.37	2,177.27
April	587.27	321.42	729.37	397.27	185.28	2,220.61
May	535.22	275.52	750.54	335.23	184.97	2,081.48
June	539.20	226.80	755.67	394.25	181.08	2,097.00
Total	$3,175.53	$1,479.64	$4,418.42	$2,444.88	$1,052.37	$12,570.84

35. On the basis of the above chart, the TOTAL expenses of the dental clinic exceed the total expenses of the baby clinic for the six-month period by 35.____

    A. $1,242.89   B. $1,243.79   C. $1,342.79   D. $1,343.89

36. The total expenses for the month of January for Health Center X EXCEED the total expenses of the chest clinic for the six-month period by 36.____

    A. $473.82   B. $483.72   C. $484.72   D. $493.72

37. The expenditures for the entire Health Center were HIGHEST during the month of 37.____

    A. February   B. March   C. April   D. June

38. If the total number of patients treated at the Health Center during February was 632, the APPROXIMATE cost per patient for the month of February is 38.____

    A. $3.20   B. $12.50   C. $21.00   D. $31.90

39. The TOTAL expenditure for the dental clinic for the six-month period is 39.____

    A. *more* than double the total expenses of the Health Center for March
    B. *less* than one-fourth the total expenses of the Health Center for the six-month period
    C. *more* than double the total expenses of the Health Center for April
    D. *less* than the combined totals for the six-month period of expenses for the baby and x-ray clinics

40. The TOTAL expenditure for the first three months for the baby clinic is 40.____

    A. *greater* than the total expenses for the baby clinic for the last three months
    B. *less* than the total expenses for the chest clinic for the entire six-month period
    C. *less* than the total expenses for the baby clinic for the last three months
    D. *greater* than the total expenses for the pre-natal clinic for the entire six-month period

KEY (CORRECT ANSWERS)

1. B	11. C	21. B	31. C
2. A	12. D	22. C	32. B
3. C	13. B	23. A	33. D
4. B	14. D	24. D	34. C
5. D	15. C	25. A	35. A
6. C	16. D	26. D	36. D
7. D	17. A	27. C	37. C
8. A	18. C	28. D	38. A
9. B	19. B	29. B	39. A
10. C	20. C	30. B	40. C

TEST 2

DIRECTIONS: Each question or incomplete statement is followed by several suggested answers or completions. Select the one that BEST answers the question or completes the statement. *PRINT THE LETTER OF THE CORRECT ANSWER IN THE SPACE AT THE RIGHT.*

1. For an employee to address callers at the clinic by name is   1._____

   A. *advisable;* this is a courtesy that everyone appreciates
   B. *inadvisable;* it would be very embarrassing if she greeted a patient by the wrong name
   C. *advisable;* this assures the patient that the assistant is concentrating on her work
   D. *inadvisable;* patients will tend to take advantage of this display of familiarity

2. One of your duties is to get certain preliminary information from a new patient before giving him or her an appointment with the doctor for a later day. The data are to be entered on a permanent record card. Assume that you are interviewing a woman who speaks very broken English and asks if she can talk to you in Spanish. You speak some Spanish and are able to get most of the information from her, but are unable to understand a few of her answers.   2._____
   The one of the following which is the BEST action for you to take is to

   A. tell the woman you can't understand her and ask her to come back with an interpreter
   B. fill in on the card all the necessary data as best you can
   C. fill in the information you are certain to have understood correctly, and, at the time of the next appointment, point out to the doctor the omissions
   D. write out for the woman the questions you have not answered on the card and ask her to bring back the answers in writing, in English, the next time she comes

3. Assume that the doctor who is to take charge of the morning session of your clinic has been unavoidably detained and arrives an hour late, at 10 A.M.   3._____
   The one of the following which is the BEST action for you to take is to

   A. ask the patients who have arrived for the appointment between 9 and 10:00 to come back at another time
   B. ask all patients if they can wait; if not, give them appointments for another time
   C. say nothing to any of the patients
   D. ask the patients who had appointments for the last hour of the session to come back at another time

4. Assume that you are put in charge of a medicine supply cabinet and you note two identical bottles, one containing a harmless liquid, the other a poisonous substance. You should   4._____

   A. make certain that both bottles are clearly labeled at all times
   B. make certain that the bottle containing the poisonous substance is clearly labeled at all times
   C. pour the liquids over into different shaped bottles
   D. keep the bottles on two different shelves

9

2 (#2)

5. Assume that a patient with a painful shoulder comes in during the doctor's absence and asks you to give him a treatment such as the doctor had prescribed for him some months earlier.
You should

    A. comply with the request since the difficulty is obviously a relapse
    B. give the patient a sedative and suggest that he call for a future appointment if the pain does not subside
    C. ask him to return later when the doctor will be in
    D. explain that, since you are not a registered nurse, you are not qualified to give treatment

5._____

6. A patient telephones the clinic before the doctor arrives and says that the medicine the doctor prescribed for her makes her nauseous. She wants to know whether she should continue taking it.
The one of the following steps which you should take FIRST is to

    A. advise her to stop taking the medication if it is not effective
    B. suggest that she continue taking the medicine for another week to see if the nausea stops
    C. say that you will inform the doctor and call her back
    D. recommend that she check the accuracy of the prescription with the pharmacist

6._____

7. Assume that one of the medicines in your supply cabinet is one which deteriorates within a certain period of time, and becomes ineffective after that time. According to instructions, you reorder the medicine periodically, so that when the old supply becomes ineffective a fresh supply is on hand. You find, however, that only a small quantity from each bottle is being used, and the major portion has to be thrown away.
The one of the following which is the BEST procedure for you to follow is to

    A. continue to order as before, since you cannot prevent the medicine from spoiling
    B. wait with the fresh order until the old supply has been used up
    C. order periodically as before, but in smaller quantities
    D. order periodically, but at greater intervals, so that more of the medicine will be used up

7._____

8. Assume that you are charged with the weekly weighing of a certain group of children attending your clinic. Your doctor instructs you to fill out a certain card form for any child whose weight differs by 5% or more from the previous week's reading. One morning, you weigh five of these children. Child A weighs 63 lbs., B, 54 lbs., C, 47 1/2 lbs., D, 57 lbs., and E, 61 lbs. The previous week's readings were: A, 65 lbs.; B, 51 lbs.; C, 50 lbs.; D, 59 1/2 lbs.; E, 56 1/2 lbs.
The children for whom you will make out cards will be

    A. A, B, and C   B. B and E
    C. A, C, D, and E   D. B, C, and E

8._____

9. A mother comes to the health center with an infant who appears to be ill. As she comes in, she tells you she believes the child may have caught the measles from a neighbor's child who is just recovering from the disease. The BEST of the following actions for you to take is to

    A. tell the mother to take a seat and wait her turn to see the doctor

9._____

10

B. ask the mother if she wants to take a chance on a cancelled appointment, as the doctor's schedule is filled for the day
C. scold the mother for coming in without an appointment and arrange for an appointment on the next clinic day
D. take the mother and child into a vacant examination room and inform the doctor at once

10. Assume that you notice that one of the drugs in your supply cabinet has changed color. It is not on the list of drugs which deteriorate and which must be reordered periodically. The one of the following which is the BEST action for you to take is to

    A. order a new supply of the drug immediately
    B. report the matter to the doctor immediately
    C. ignore the change in the drug, as it is not caused by deterioration
    D. point out the change to the doctor the next time he asks for the drug

11. To use screw caps on medicine bottles in preference to glass stoppers is

    A. *wise*; screw caps are more attractive
    B. *unwise*; glass stoppers are less expensive
    C. *wise*; screw caps afford more protection to the lip of the bottle
    D. *unwise*; glass stoppers are often interchangeable for several bottles

12. The one of the following which is the LEAST important precaution to take in connection with the pouring of a dose of medicine from a bottle into a glass is to

    A. wear sterile rubber gloves while pouring
    B. hold the label on the bottle uppermost while pouring
    C. clean the rim of the bottle after pouring
    D. make certain the medicine isn't left around for any time in an unmarked glass

13. To cover a typed label on a medicine bottle with shellac is

    A. *inadvisable*; the shellac may have a chemical reaction on the drug
    B. *advisable*; the label will become waterproof and the printing on it remain legible
    C. *inadvisable*; the shellac will cause the printing on the label to become illegible
    D. *advisable*; the shellac will prevent the bottle from breaking in case it is dropped

14. The one of the following which is the MOST valid reason for a patient's needing a prescription in order to obtain a certain drug is that the drug is

    A. poisonous   B. habit-forming
    C. expensive   D. potent

15. While a growing health consciousness is apparent here and in many other countries, our knowledge of how to prevent and control disease far exceeds its application. This statement means MOST NEARLY that

    A. much of our knowledge of how to improve public health is not put into practice
    B. there has been little increase in our knowledge of disease prevention and control
    C. some of our knowledge on control of diseases is impossible to put into practice
    D. there has been no improvement in the prevention and control of disease

16. Developments in the field of nutrition have been an important part of medical progress. Not only have dietary cures been discovered for true nutritional diseases but, in almost every branch of medicine and surgery, therapy has been improved by more scientific methods of feeding. The one of the following which is the MOST accurate statement on the basis of the above paragraph is that

    A. nutrition plays a minor role in medicine
    B. dietary cures have therapeutic values only in cases of nutritional diseases
    C. proper nutrition is important in the cure of diseases in almost every branch of medicine
    D. nutritional diseases can be cured only by special diets

17. An individual may be wholly immune to one disease and ultra-susceptible to another; and such immunity, which may be born with the individual or acquired, has absolutely no relation to physique, robustness, or great vitality. The one of the following which is the MOST accurate statement on the basis of this paragraph is that

    A. an adult who is immune to a disease must have been immune to that disease as a child
    B. a person who is susceptible to one disease has a tendency to be susceptible to all diseases
    C. a person of poor physique and low vitality may nevertheless be immune to certain diseases
    D. persons of low vitality are more susceptible to diseases than persons of great vitality

18. If the doctor is in consultation with another doctor, he should not be disturbed. As used in this sentence, the word *consultation* means MOST NEARLY

    A. conference   B. operation   C. agreement   D. argument

19. A nurse should not prescribe for patients without the doctor's instructions. As used in this sentence, the word *prescribe* means MOST NEARLY

    A. explain the cuases of illness
    B. ascertain the case history
    C. determine the appointment time
    D. recommend treatment

20. The doctor has the right to refer patients to the hospital. As used in this sentence, the word *refer* means MOST NEARLY

    A. accept   B. admit   C. direct   D. accompany

21. An antidote is an agent which

    A. allays pain
    B. counteracts the effects of a poison
    C. reduces acidity
    D. stimulates the heart

22. Physical therapy has an important place in medicine. As used in this sentence, the word *therapy* means MOST NEARLY

    A. massage   B. treatment   C. exercise   D. examination

23. Doctors must not advertise or in any way solicit patients. As used in this sentence, the word *solicit* means MOST NEARLY

    A. actively seek B. greet
    C. exploit D. deliberately hurt

24. After examining the patient, the doctor indicated the prognosis of the illness. As used in this sentence, the word *prognosis* means MOST NEARLY

    A. probable course B. cause
    C. treatment D. past history

25. A doctor practicing *obstetrics* deals with

    A. glandular disorders B. deformities of the bones
    C. pregnancy D. children's diseases

26. The patient's condition was aggravated by a severe case of phobia. The word *phobia* means MOST NEARLY

    A. fever B. apathy
    C. indigestion D. fear

27. Neglect of immediate treatment may cause an illness to become chronic. The word *chronic* means MOST NEARLY

    A. incurable B. painful
    C. prolonged D. contagious

28. The one of the following which is NOT generally used to alleviate pain is

    A. aspirin B. morphine C. cocaine D. quinine

29. The administration of a drug subcutaneously means administration by

    A. mouth
    B. injection beneath the skin
    C. application on the surface of the skin
    D. rectum

30. The one of the following which is NOT a disinfectant is

    A. boiling water B. iodine
    C. formaldehyde D. novocain

31. The one of the following which is LEAST related to the pulse rate of an individual is his

    A. blood pressure B. temperature
    C. weight D. emotional state

32. The one of the following which denotes normal vision is

    A. 20/10 B. 20/20 C. 20/30 D. 20/40

33. Of the following, the temperature which is MOST desirable for a babies' weighing room in a health center is _____ ° F.

    A. 60-62 B. 65-68 C. 75-77 D. 85-88

34. Of the following, it is MOST advisable for the operator to wear dark glasses during treatments by

    A. x-ray
    B. infrared radiation
    C. diathermy
    D. ultraviolet radiation

35. Of the following, the BEST method of sterilizing glassware for surgical purposes is by means of

    A. immersion in boiling water
    B. steaming under pressure
    C. cold sterilization
    D. washing thoroughly with soap and water

36. The apparatus used for sterilizing medical equipment by means of steam under pressure is the

    A. autoclave   B. manometer   C. catheter   D. reamer

37. After each use of a thermometer, it should be

    A. held under hot water for several minutes
    B. disinfected in a chemical solution
    C. rinsed in cold water
    D. wiped clean with cotton

38. The LEAST desirable action to take in administering first aid to a person suffering from shock is to

    A. give the patient some aromatic spirits of ammonia
    B. place the patient in a reclining position and elevate his legs
    C. loosen any tight clothing and place a pillow under his head
    D. place a hot water bottle near the patient's feet

39. Of the following symptoms, the one which does NOT generally accompany a fainting spell is

    A. a flushed face
    B. perspiration of the forehead
    C. shallow breathing
    D. a slow pulse

40. Assume that a six-year-old boy is brought to the clinic, bleeding profusely from a scalp wound. The doctor has not as yet arrived.
    Of the following, the MOST effective action for you to take is to

    A. wash the wound thoroughly with soap and water to prevent infection; apply pressure on the bleeding point; then treat for shock
    B. place the boy in a comfortable position; apply tincture of iodine to the wound to prevent infection; then treat for shock
    C. give the patient a stimulant; then attempt to stop the bleeding by applying digital pressure
    D. make the boy comfortable; place a compress over the wound and bandage snugly; then threat for shock

41. Of the following, the MOST frequently used method for the diagnosis of pulmonary tuberculosis is the

    A. blood test
    B. x-ray
    C. metabolism test
    D. urinalysis

42. Of the following conditions, the one which may be infectious is

    A. diabetes
    B. tuberculosis
    C. appendicitis
    D. hypertension

43. Of the following, observation of deviations from normal body weight may aid LEAST in determining the presence of

    A. glandular disturbances
    B. malnutrition
    C. organic disturbances
    D. mental deficiency

44. Leukemia is a disease of the blood characterized by a

    A. moderate increase in the red cell count and decrease in the white cell count
    B. marked decrease in the red cell count and an increase in the white cell count
    C. marked increase in the hemoglobin content
    D. marked decrease in the white cell count

45. The one of the following which is MOST commonly used in the treatment of arthritis is

    A. radium
    B. an electrocardiogram
    C. a radiograph
    D. diathermy

46. The fluoroscope is used CHIEFLY to

    A. provide a permanent picture of the condition of internal organs at a given time
    B. make a chart of the action of the muscles of the heart
    C. observe the internal structure and functioning of the organs of the body at a given time
    D. produce heat in the tissues of the body

47. A stethoscope is an instrument used for

    A. determining the blood pressure
    B. taking the body temperature
    C. chest examination
    D. determining the amount of sugar in the blood

48. The Dick test is used to determine susceptibility to

   A. measles B. scarlet fever
   C. diphtheria D. chickenpox

49. The aorta is a(n)

   A. bone   B. artery   C. ligament   D. nerve

50. The esophagus is part of the

   A. alimentary canal B. abdominal wall
   C. mucous membrane D. circulatory system

51. Of the following, the one which is NOT a blood vessel is the

   A. vein   B. capillary   C. ganglion   D. artery

52. Vital statistics include data reflating to

   A. births, deaths, and marriages
   B. the cost of food, clothing, and shelter
   C. the number of children per family unit
   D. diseases and their comparative mortality rates

53. In filing letters by subject, you should be MOST concerned with the

   A. name of the sender
   B. main topic of the letter
   C. date of the correspondence
   D. alphabetic cross reference

54. When arranging the record cards of patients in alphabetical order, the one of the following which should be filed THIRD is

   A. Charles A. Clarke B. James Clark
   C. Joan Carney D. Mae Cohen

55. The one of the following names which should be filed FIRST is

   A. Benjamin Dermody B. Frank Davidson
   C. Matthew Davids D. Seymour Diana

Questions 56-60.

DIRECTIONS: Questions 56 through 60 are to be answered on the basis of the chart below.

ATTENDANCE OF PATIENTS AT Y HEALTH CENTER
FOR WEEK OF APRIL 10

Clinic	Number Summoned for				Number Reported to			
	Baby	Chest	Eye	V.D.	Baby	Chest	Eye	V.D.
Monday	30	42	36	38	29	40	33	35
Tuesday	33	29	34	37	30	29	31	36
Wednesday	38	31	45	42	35	30	40	40
Thursday	41	48	41	32	36	45	39	28
Friday	35	37	39	36	33	35	37	32

56. On the basis of the above chart, it is CORRECT to say that

    A. more patients were summoned to the baby clinic than to the chest clinic during the week
    B. the same number of patients were absent from the eye clinic and the baby clinic during the week
    C. more patients reported to the eye clinic than to the chest clinic during the week
    D. more patients were summoned to the V.D. clinic than to the eye clinic during the week

57. On the basis of the above chart, the daily average number of patients summoned to the eye clinic exceeds the daily average reporting to the eye clinic by

    A. 3   B. 7   C. 11   D. 15

58. The percentage of all patients summoned to Y Health Center on Thursday who failed to report for their appointments is

    A. *less* than 5%
    B. *more* than 5% but less than 10%
    C. *more* than 10% but less than 15%
    D. *more* than 15%

59. The number of patients summoned for the entire week to the eye clinic exceeds the number of patients summoned to the baby clinic by

    A. 6   B. 9   C. 13   D. 18

60. The total number of patients who reported to Y Health Center for the week is

    A. 683   B. 693   C. 724   D. 744

Questions 61-80.

DIRECTIONS: Column I below lists words used in medical practice. Column II lists phrases which describe the words in Column I. In the space at the right, place the letter preceding the phrase in Column II which BEST describes the word in Column I.

COLUMN I	COLUMN II
61. Abrasion	A. A disturbance of digestion
62. Aseptic	B. Destroying the germs of disease
63. Cardiac	C. A general poisoning of the blood
64. Catarrh	D. An instrument used for injecting fluids
65. Contamination	E. A scraping off of the skin
66. Dermatology	F. Free from disease germs
67. Disinfectant	G. An apparatus for viewing internal organs by means of x-rays
68. Dyspepsia	H. An instrument for assisting the eye in observing minute objects
69. Epidemic	I. An inoculable immunizing agent
70. Epidermis	J. The extensive prevalence in a community of a disease
71. Incubation	K. Chemical product of an organ
72. Microscope	L. Preceding birth
73. Pediatrics	M. Fever
74. Plasma	N. The branch of medical science that relates to the skin and its diseases
75. Prenatal	O. Fluid part of the blood
76. Retina	P. The science of the hygienic care of children
77. Syphilis	Q. Infection by contact
78. Syringe	R. Relating to the heart
79. Toxemia	S. Inner structure of the eye
80. Vaccine	T. Outer portion of the skin
	U. Pertaining to the ductless gland
	V. An infectious venereal disease
	W. Pertaining to the hip
	X. The development of an infectious disease from the period of infection to that of the appearance of the first symptoms
	Y. Simple inflammation of a mucous membrane
	Z. An instrument for measuring blood pressure

61. ____
62. ____
63. ____
64. ____
65. ____
66. ____
67. ____
68. ____
69. ____
70. ____
71. ____
72. ____
73. ____
74. ____
75. ____
76. ____
77. ____
78. ____
79. ____
80. ____

KEY (CORRECT ANSWERS)

1. A	16. C	31. C	46. C	61. E	76. S
2. D	17. C	32. B	47. C	62. F	77. V
3. B	18. A	33. C	48. B	63. R	78. D
4. A	19. D	34. D	49. B	64. Y	79. C
5. C	20. C	35. B	50. A	65. Q	80. I
6. C	21. B	36. A	51. C	66. N	
7. C	22. B	37. B	52. A	67. B	
8. D	23. A	38. C	53. B	68. A	
9. D	24. A	39. A	54. A	69. J	
10. B	25. C	40. D	55. C	70. T	
11. C	26. D	41. B	56. C	71. X	
12. A	27. C	42. B	57. A	72. H	
13. B	28. D	43. D	58. B	73. P	
14. B	29. B	44. B	59. D	74. O	
15. A	30. D	45. D	60. B	75. L	

EXAMINATION SECTION
TEST 1

DIRECTIONS: Each question or incomplete statement is followed by several suggested answers or completions. Select the one that BEST answers the question or completes the statement. *PRINT THE LETTER OF THE CORRECT ANSWER IN THE SPACE AT THE RIGHT.*

1. Assume that you are assigned to a health center. A middle-aged man walks in and says that he doesn't feel well. He complains of a slight pain in the chest and has difficulty breathing.
   Of the following actions, the one you should take is to

   A. isolate him immediately as he may have *Asian flu*
   B. find out what he has eaten as he may have food poisoning
   C. ask him to sit down and see if he can catch his breath
   D. see that he is seated and then call a doctor

   1.____

2. A baby who has been brought to the health center for an examination has been crying continuously for 20 minutes. The BEST of the following actions you should take is to

   A. have the baby examined by the first available physician
   B. ask the others who are waiting if they would object to the baby being examined out of turn
   C. call the situation to the attention of the nurse in charge
   D. do nothing as there are probably others who are ill and need to see the doctor

   2.____

3. Suppose that a mother comes into the health center, carrying a 3-year-old child who is ill. The mother tells you that the child has a temperature of 102°F, his nose is stuffed, and he is sneezing.
   For you to seat the mother and child apart from the others who are waiting for the physician is

   A. *correct;* the other children and adults in the clinic should not be exposed to a disease which may be contagious
   B. *incorrect;* the mother might be offended if she were treated differently than the other patients
   C. *correct;* the nurse is in a good position to diagnose patients when the doctor is not available
   D. *incorrect;* you should wait until the physician makes his diagnosis before isolating the child

   3.____

4. In the performance of her work, it is not enough that the employee be alert to the immediate demands of her own job; she must be constantly aware of the basic function of the clinic.
   This statement means that a worker should view the ultimate purpose of her job as

   A. giving effective service to patients
   B. getting the most work done in the shortest time
   C. following to the letter all orders given to her
   D. reporting punctually and working diligently

   4.____

21

5. While serving at an eye clinic, you are instructed to answer the phone by saying, *Eye Clinic, Miss Jones speaking.*
   Of the following, the BEST reason for this practice is that

   A. it sets the tone for a brief, concise telephone conversation
   B. it is the standard practice recommended by the telephone company and is familiar to callers
   C. the caller will understand that he cannot ask for medical information, since you are not a physician
   D. the caller will know whether he is speaking to the person he wants to reach

6. If a telephone call is received for a doctor while he is examining a patient, it would be BEST to

   A. tell the caller to telephone again when the doctor can receive a call
   B. take the caller's telephone number and have the doctor return the call when he is free
   C. ask the nature of the call in order to determine if it requires the doctor's immediate attention
   D. refer the call to the nurse in charge as she may have the information the caller requires

7. Suppose that a patient who attends the clinic has made frequent complaints, usually unjustified.
   Of the following, the BEST reason for not ignoring another complaint from her is that

   A. she is likely to take her complaint to a higher level
   B. even though past complaints have been unjustified, this particular one may require attention
   C. a patient is often pacified if you pretend that you will look into her complaint
   D. no distinction should be made in your attitude toward patients

8. Clinic appointments are less likely to be broken if you

   A. make appointments on dates which are convenient for the patients
   B. stress to each patient that a broken appointment inconveniences other patients
   C. threaten not to make any more appointments for patients who break appointments without a good reason
   D. arrange the schedule of appointments so that patients do not have to wait in the clinic

9. Assume that every day the schedule of the clinic is severely disrupted because several patients without appointments must be treated for emergency conditions. Of the following, the BEST suggestion you could make in order to minimize disruption is that

   A. one morning a week be set aside when all emergency cases will be treated
   B. applicants who claim emergency conditions be screened to see which of them really need emergency treatment
   C. unassigned periods be allowed in the schedule in anticipation of emergency cases
   D. the clinic be kept open each evening until all patients have been treated

10. Suppose that a woman who is scheduled to appear at 3:30 P.M. comes into the clinic at 10 A.M. and says she is ill and must see the doctor at once. The clinic is already quite crowded.
It would be BEST for you to

    A. try to determine if she is really ill, since some patients use the claim as a ruse to get prompt attention
    B. tell her to return at the proper time, since the other patients will become disorderly if others are taken before they are
    C. see if the head nurse will take her out of turn, since she may need prompt care
    D. see if a clinic physician is willing to see her, since public reaction would be hostile if the condition of the woman became worse while waiting

10.____

11. Some authorities advocate that the mother not stay in the same room when a child of 3 or 4 is being treated by the doctor.
Of the following, the BEST reason for this is that the

    A. mother might become upset if she watches the treatment
    B. child is less likely to accept the doctor's authority
    C. mother will prolong the examination by questioning the doctor about her child
    D. child will mature more rapidly if he is not always accompanied by his mother

11.____

12. Assume that a patient tells you that he is not going to follow the treatment recommended by the physician because he doesn't have long to live anyway.
It would be BEST for you to

    A. report the conversation to the physician
    B. point out to the patient that it is foolish to come for treatment if he will not follow the recommendations given him by the physician
    C. explain to the patient that he will live longer and less painfully if he follows the physician's recommendations
    D. try to get a relative in whom the patient has confidence to persuade him to follow the physician's recommendations

12.____

13. Suppose that a patient who has just received treatment in the clinic complains loudly that she was kept waiting a lone time and then received hasty and inadequate treatment.
It is BEST for you to

    A. explain that treatment is necessarily hasty because the clinic is busy
    B. avoid arguing with her, since ill people are often overwrought
    C. tell her she is not qualified to decide whether treatment is adequate
    D. refer the patient back to the physician for completion of treatment

13.____

14. Assume that a patient who has been coming to the clinic for some time asks you, *Do I have a heart condition?* You know that his clinic record card bears the notation *heart murmur.*
Under these circumstances, it would be BEST for you to tell him

    A. he has a heart murmur, since he obviously knows this and his card gives you the information
    B. he does not have a heart condition, since the doctor would have informed the patient if he wanted him to know about it

14.____

C. not to worry about it since lots of people have a heart condition
D. to ask the physician whom he has been seeing in the clinic about this

15. If a 3-year-old child refuses to stay on a scale long enough to be weighed, the BEST of the following actions for you to take is to

    A. obtain the child's weight by first weighing the mother holding the child in her arms, and then weighing the mother alone
    B. insist that the child be weighed so that the other children in the clinic will cooperate when being weighed
    C. ask one of the special officers to assist her in weighing the child
    D. note on the record that the child refused to be weighed and let the physician determine if it is necessary to weigh the child

16. You have been asked to hand the sterile instruments to the physician while he is changing a dressing. Suppose that halfway through the procedure, the doctor drops the forceps he is using.
    Of the following actions, the one that you should take at this time is to

    A. pick up the forceps with your hand and ask the doctor if he will need it any more
    B. pick up the forceps with your hand and place it with other contaminated instruments
    C. move the forceps out of the way with your foot
    D. use sterile forceps from the cabinet to pick up the forceps from the floor

17. You have been asked to prepare a list of supplies to be reordered for your clinic.
    In order for you to determine how much of any item to reorder, it would be MOST important to know

    A. the average amount of the item used in a given period of time
    B. what the item is used for in the clinic
    C. how much storage space is available for these supplies
    D. the cost of each item

18. Assume that when you open a cabinet in which disinfectants are kept, you find that one of the bottles has no label. However, there is a label on the shelf near the bottle.
    Of the following, the BEST action for you to take is to

    A. paste the label on the bottle since it obviously is the label for that bottle
    B. paste the label on the bottle only if the label has the word *disinfectant* clearly marked on it
    C. place the bottle back in the cabinet and ask the nurse in charge what to do
    D. pour the contents of the bottle into the sink, rinse the bottle, and place it in the proper receptacle

19. After washing and rinsing rubber hot water bottles, hang then upside down with their mouths open. When they are thoroughly dry, inflate them, place the stoppers into the mouths of the bottles, and leave them hanging. If they are to be stored, leave them inflated and place gauze or crushed paper between them.
    On the basis of this paragraph, the one of the following statements that is MOST accurate is that, when storing hot water bottles,

A. they should be stuffed with paper
B. a free flow of air must circulate around them
C. care must be taken to prevent their sides from sticking together
D. they should be placed upside down with their mouths open

20. In filing, a cross index should be used for a record which

    A. may be filed in either of two places
    B. has been temporarily removed from the file
    C. concerns a patient who is no longer coming to the clinic
    D. will be used to remind patients of appointments

21. Assume that the cards of patients are kept in alphabetical order. You are given an alphabetical list of persons who have received injections for *Asian flu* at the clinic, and are asked to see if there is a card in the file for each person on the list.
    It would be BEST for you to

    A. determine if the number of cards and the number of names on the list are the same
    B. place a check mark next to each name on the list for which there is a corresponding card
    C. place a check mark on each card for which there is a corresponding name on the list
    D. prepare a second list of all cards in the file and place a check mark next to each name for which there is a corresponding name on the first list

22. Assume that there are several clinics within a health center. Patients' cards are filed according to the clinic which they attend, and within each clinic are filed alphabetically. Every Friday you are responsible for filing the cards of all patients who were in the health center during that week. The cards are in mixed order.
    Of the following, the FIRST step to take is to

    A. arrange the patients' cards in alphabetical order
    B. separate the cards of those patients who attended more than one clinic from all the others
    C. arrange the patients' cards according to the clinic attended
    D. arrange the patients' cards according to the date the patient attended the clinic

23. Suppose that, in Clinic A, a medical history card is prepared for each new patient. In this clinic, a blood test is made for each patient as a routine procedure. You have been instructed to make out either a blue card for a negative report, or a white card for a positive report, when the laboratory reports of the blood tests are received.
    In order to make sure that all reports on the blood tests have been received, you should compare the number of reports received with the number of _____ cards.

    A. medical history   B. blue
    C. white   D. blue and white

24. Assume that you are in charge of ordering supplies needed for the clinic. When reordering items, it is BEST to

A. count supplies at the beginning of each month and reorder an item as soon as there is no more of it in stock
B. determine beforehand the amount of each item which it is necessary to have on hand and reorder the item when the supply falls to this level
C. reorder each item in sufficient quantity to last half a year so that there will be no danger of running out of supplies
D. reorder all items at the beginning of each month so that no item needed will be forgotten

25. It is usually recommended that, when new supplies of any item are received, they be placed beneath or behind supplies of the item already in stock.
Of the following, the BEST reason for this is that this procedure

    A. requires less frequent handling of supplies
    B. makes it easier to tell how much of each item you have on hand
    C. allows you to use the storage space most effectively
    D. makes it more likely that the older supplies will be used first

26. The abbreviation *EEG* refers to a(n)

    A. examination of the eyes and ears
    B. inflammatory disease of the urinogenital tract
    C. disease of the esophageal structure
    D. examination of the brain

27. The complete destruction of all forms of living microorganisms is called

    A. decontamination   B. fumigation
    C. sterilization   D. germination

28. A rectal thermometer differs from other fever thermometers in that it has a

    A. longer stem   B. thinner stem
    C. stubby bulb at one end D. slender bulb at one end

29. The one of the following pieces of equipment which is usually used together with a sphygmometer is a

    A. stethoscope   B. watch
    C. fever thermometer   D. hypodermic syringe

30. A curette is a

    A. healing drug   B. curved scalpel
    C. long hypodermic needle D. scraping instrument

31. The otoscope is used to examine the patient's

    A. eyes   B. ears   C. mouth   D. lungs

32. A catheter is used

    A. to close wounds
    B. for withdrawing fluid from a body cavity
    C. to remove cataracts
    D. as a cathartic

33. Of the following pieces of equipment, the one that is required for making a scratch test is a

    A. needle
    B. scalpel
    C. capillary tube
    D. tourniquet

34. A hemostat is an instrument which is used to

    A. hold a sterile needle
    B. clamp off a blood vessel
    C. regulate the temperature of a sterilizer
    D. measure oxygen intake

35. Of the following medical supplies, the one that MUST be stored in a tightly sealed bottle is

    A. sodium fluoride
    B. alum
    C. oil of cloves
    D. aromatic spirits of ammonia

36. A person who has been exposed to an infectious disease is called

    A. a contact
    B. an incubator
    C. diseased
    D. infected

37. A myocardial infarct would occur in the

    A. heart   B. kidneys   C. lungs   D. spleen

38. The abbreviations *WBC* and *RBC* refer to the results of tests of the

    A. basal metabolism
    B. blood
    C. blood pressure
    D. bony structure

39. When a person's blood pressure is noted as 120/80, it means that his _____ blood pressure is _____.

    A. pulse; 120
    B. pulse; 80
    C. systolic; 120
    D. systolic; 80

40. The anatomical structure that contains the tonsils and adenoids is the

    A. pharynx   B. larynx   C. trachea   D. sinuses

41. An abscess can BEST be described as a

    A. loss of sensation
    B. painful tooth
    C. ruptured membrane
    D. localized formation of pus

42. Nephritis is a disease affecting the

    A. gall bladder
    B. larynx
    C. kidney
    D. large intestine

43. Hemoglobin is contained in the

    A. white blood cells
    B. lymph fluids
    C. platelets
    D. red blood cells

44. Bile is a body fluid that is MOST directly concerned with

    A. digestion
    B. excretion
    C. reproduction
    D. metabolism

45. Of the following bones, the one which is located below the waist is the

    A. sternum   B. clavicle   C. tibia   D. humerus

46. The one of the following which is NOT part of the digestive canal is the

    A. esophagus   B. larynx   C. duodenum   D. colon

47. The thyroid and the pituitary are part of the _____ system.

    A. digestive
    B. endocrine
    C. respiratory
    D. excretory

48. The one of the following which would be included in a *GU* examination is the

    A. rectum   B. trachea   C. kidneys   D. pancreas

49. Of the following, the one which would be included in the x-ray examination known as a *GI series* is the

    A. colon   B. skull   C. lungs   D. uterus

50. A person who, while not ill himself, may transmit a disease to another person is known as a(n)

    A. breeder
    B. incubator
    C. carrier
    D. inhibitor

KEY (CORRECT ANSWERS)

1. D	11. B	21. B	31. B	41. D
2. C	12. A	22. C	32. B	42. C
3. A	13. B	23. A	33. A	43. D
4. A	14. D	24. B	34. B	44. A
5. D	15. A	25. D	35. D	45. C
6. C	16. C	26. D	36. A	46. B
7. B	17. A	27. C	37. A	47. B
8. A	18. D	28. C	38. B	48. C
9. C	19. C	29. A	39. C	49. A
10. C	20. A	30. D	40. A	50. C

TEST 2

DIRECTIONS: Each question or incomplete statement is followed by several suggested answers or completions. Select the one that BEST answers the question or completes the statement. *PRINT THE LETTER OF THE CORRECT ANSWER IN THE SPACE AT THE RIGHT.*

1. Thorough washing of the hands for two minutes with soap and warm water will leave the hands   1.____

   A. sterile
   B. aseptic
   C. decontaminated
   D. partially disinfected

2. The one of the following which is BEST for preparing the skin for an injection is   2.____

   A. green soap and water
   B. alcohol
   C. phenol
   D. formalin

3. A fever thermometer should be cleansed after use by washing it with   3.____

   A. soap and cool water
   B. warm water only
   C. soap and hot water
   D. running cold tap water

4. The FIRST step in cleaning an instrument which has fresh blood on it is to   4.____

   A. wash it in hot soapy water
   B. wash it under cool running water
   C. soak it in a boric acid bath
   D. soak it in 70% alcohol

5. If a contaminated nasal speculum cannot be sterilized immediately after use, then the BEST procedure to follow until sterilization is possible is to place it   5.____

   A. under a piece of dry gauze
   B. in warm water
   C. in alcohol
   D. in a green soap solution

6. A hypodermic needle should always be checked to see if it has a good sharp point   6.____

   A. when it is being washed
   B. when it is removed from the sterilizer
   C. just before it is sterilized
   D. immediately before an injection

7. Of the following, the LOWEST temperature at which cotton goods will be sterilized if placed in an autoclave for 30 minutes is _____ °F.   7.____

   A. 130   B. 170   C. 200   D. 250

8. Of the following procedures, the one which is BEST for sterilizing an ear speculum which is contaminated with wax is to   8.____

29

A. scrub in with cold soapy water, rinse in ether, and place in boiling water for 20 minutes
B. soak it in warm water, scrub in cold soapy water, rinse with water, and autoclave at 275°F for 10 minutes
C. wash it in alcohol, scrub in hot soapy water, rinse with water, and place in boiling water for 20 minutes
D. wash it in 1% Lysol solution, rinse, and autoclave at 275°F for 15 minutes

9. Assume that clean water accidentally spilled on the outside of a package of cloth-wrapped hypodermic syringes which has been sterilized.
Of the following, the BEST action to take is to

    A. leave the package to dry in a sunny, clean place
    B. sterilize the package again
    C. remove the wet cloth and wrap the package in a dry sterile cloth
    D. wipe off the package with a clean dry towel and later ask the nurse in charge what to do

10. Hypodermic needles should be sterilized by placing them in

    A. boiling water for 5 minutes
    B. an autoclave at 15 lbs. pressure for 15 minutes
    C. oil heated to 220°F for 10 minutes
    D. a 1:40 Lysol solution for 10 minutes

11. A cutting instrument should be sterilized by placing it in

    A. a chemical germicide
    B. an autoclave at 15 lbs. pressure for 20 minutes
    C. boiling water for 20 minutes
    D. a hot air oven at 320°F for 1 hour

12. A fever thermometer used by a patient who has tuberculosis should be washed and then placed in _____ minute(s).

    A. boiling water for 10
    B. a hot air oven for 20
    C. a 1:1000 solution of bichloride of mercury for one
    D. an autoclave at 15 lbs. pressure for 15

13. The MOST reliable method of sterilizing a glass syringe is to place it in _____ minutes.

    A. Zephiran chloride 1:1000 solution for 40
    B. oil heated to 250°F for 12
    C. boiling water for 20
    D. an autoclave at 15 lbs. pressure for 20

14. The insides of sterilizers should be cleaned daily with a mild abrasive PRIMARILY to

    A. remove scale
    B. prevent the growth of bacteria
    C. remove blood and other organic matter
    D. prevent acids from damaging the sterilizer

15. Of the following, the BEST reason for giving a patient a jar in which to bring a urine specimen on his next visit to the clinic is that the

   A. patient may not have a jar at home
   B. patient may bring the specimen in a jar which is too large
   C. patient may bring the specimen in a jar which has not been cleaned properly
   D. jar may be misplaced if it is not a jar in which urine specimens are usually collected

15.____

16. Simply providing nutritional information and recommended low-cost diets to clinic patients has not resulted in improved diets for their children.
The MOST plausible conclusion to draw from this statement is that

   A. nutrition is only one factor in improving health
   B. nutrition is of greater value in improving the health of adults than in improving the health of children
   C. the health problems of clinic patients are not caused by nutritional defects
   D. clinic patients are not using the nutritional information given them

16.____

17. Many people who appear to be robust are highly susceptible to disease, and are outlived by many seemingly frail people.
Of the following, the MOST plausible conclusion which may be drawn from this statement is that

   A. physical appearance is not a reliable indicator of health
   B. frail people take better care of themselves than do robust people
   C. disease tends to strike robust people more frequently than frail people
   D. robust people tend to overexert themselves more often than frail people do

17.____

18. The skill of interviewers, the wording of questions, and the willingness of patients to respond freely to questions all affect the results of a survey. Reports of surveys of patient attitudes toward the health work of the clinic are, therefore, valueless unless we also know how the surveys were conducted. A recent report that 85% of clinic patients were satisfied with clinic service must be treated with caution; it may be that another survey would have revealed just the opposite!
On the basis of this paragraph, it is MOST accurate to conclude that

   A. survey reports have little value in determining patient attitudes
   B. contrary to a recent report, 85% of clinic patients are dissatisfied with clinic service
   C. published results of surveys may be misleading unless accompanied by knowledge of the methods used
   D. listening to the unsolicited comments of clinic patients is of greater value than questioning them directly concerning their attitudes

18.____

Questions 19-25.

DIRECTIONS: Questions 19 through 25 are to be answered on the basis of the following table

STATISTICAL REPORT OF CLINICS IN XYZ HEALTH CENTER March				
	APPOINTMENTS		PROCEDURES	
Clinic	No. of Appointments Scheduled	No. of Broken Appointments	No. of Diagnostic Procedures	No. of Surgical Procedures
A	1400	260	1910	140
B	730	160	2000	500
C	1250	250	950	130
D	540	90	400	220
E	890	140	1500	280

19. On the basis of the preceding table, the total number of appointments kept for all clinics in the health center in March is

    A. 900 B. 3910 C. 4810 D. 5710

20. The percentage of appointments kept in Clinic C during March is

    A. 5% B. 20% C. 75% D. 80%

21. If Clinic A was open for 20 days during March, the average number of appointments scheduled each day at Clinic A is

    A. 57 B. 70 C. 140 D. 280

22. In comparison to the clinic which performed the fewest diagnostic procedures, the clinic which performed the MOST diagnostic procedures did _____ as many.

    A. twice
    C. four times
    B. three times
    D. five times

23. The average number of diagnostic procedures performed for all clinics during March is

    A. 254 B. 676 C. 1352 D. 6760

24. The percentage of all procedures done at Clinic B during March which were surgical procedures is

    A. 2% B. 2.5% C. 20% D. 25%

25. Clinic E used 10 boxes of gauze for its surgical procedures during March. If Clinic A used gauze at the same rate for its surgical procedures, the number of boxes of gauze Clinic A used during March is

    A. 3 B. 5 C. 10 D. 14

Questions 26-34.

DIRECTIONS: Each of Questions 26 through 34 consists of four words. Three of these words belong together. One word does NOT belong with the other three. For each group of words, you are to select the one word which does NOT belong with the other three words.

26.	A. conclude	B. terminate	C. initiate	D. end	26.____
27.	A. deficient C. excessive	B. inadequate D. insufficient			27.____
28.	A. rare	B. unique	C. unusual	D. frequent	28.____
29.	A. unquestionable C. doubtful	B. uncertain D. indefinite			29.____
30.	A. stretch	B. contract	C. extend	D. expand	30.____
31.	A. accelerate C. accept	B. quicken D. hasten			31.____
32.	A. sever	B. rupture	C. rectify	D. tear	32.____
33.	A. innocuous	B. injurious	C. dangerous	D. harmful	33.____
34.	A. adulterate C. taint	B. contaminate D. disinfect			34.____

Questions 35-40.

DIRECTIONS: Questions 35 through 40 are to be answered on the basis of the usual rules for alphabetical filing. For each question, indicate in the space at the right the letter preceding the name which should be filed THIRD in alphabetical order.

35.	A. Russell Cohen C. Wesley Chambers	B. Henry Cohn D. Arthur Connors	35.____
36.	A. Wanda Jenkins C. Leslie Jantzenberg	B. Pauline Jennings D. Rudy Jensen	36.____
37.	A. Arnold Wilson C. Duncan Williamson	B. Carlton Willson D. Ezra Wilston	37.____
38.	A. Joseph M. Buchman C. Constantino Brunelli	B. Gustave Bozzerman D. Armando Buccino	38.____
39.	A. Barbara Waverly C. Dennis Waterman	B. Corinne Warterdam D. Harold Wartman	39.____
40.	A. Jose Mejia C. Antonio Mejias	B. Bernard Mendelsohn D. Richard Mazzitelli	40.____

Questions 41-50.

DIRECTIONS: Questions 41 through 50 are to be answered on the basis of the usual rules of filing. Column I lists, next to the numbers 91 to 100, the names of 10 clinic patients. Column II lists, next to the letters A to D, the headings of file drawers into which you are to place the records of these patients. For each question, indicate in the space at the right the letter preceding the heading of the file drawer in which the record should be filed.

COLUMN I		COLUMN II	
41.	Frank Shea	A. Sab - Sej	41.___
42.	Rose Seaborn	B. Sek - Sio	42.___
43.	Samuel Smollin	C. Sip - Soo	43.___
44.	Thomas Shur	D. Sop - Syz	44.___
45.	Ben Schaefer		45.___
46.	Shirley Strauss		46.___
47.	Harry Spiro		47.___
48.	Dora Skelly		48.___
49.	Sylvia Smith		49.___
50.	Arnold Selz		50.___

KEY (CORRECT ANSWERS)

1.	D	11.	A	21.	B	31.	C	41.	B
2.	B	12.	C	22.	D	32.	C	42.	A
3.	A	13.	D	23.	C	33.	A	43.	C
4.	B	14.	A	24.	C	34.	D	44.	B
5.	D	15.	C	25.	B	35.	B	45.	A
6.	C	16.	D	26.	C	36.	B	46.	D
7.	D	17.	A	27.	C	37.	A	47.	D
8.	C	18.	C	28.	D	38.	D	48.	C
9.	B	19.	B	29.	A	39.	C	49.	C
10.	B	20.	D	30.	B	40.	C	50.	B

EXAMINATION SECTION
TEST 1

DIRECTIONS: Each question or incomplete statement is followed by several suggested answers or completions. Select the one that BEST answers the question or completes the statement. *PRINT THE LETTER OF THE CORRECT ANSWER IN THE SPACE AT THE RIGHT.*

1. An employee should know not only the details of his own job but the main objective of the organization for which he works.
   The MAIN objective of a health center may BEST be described as the

   A. orderly and efficient management of the health center
   B. improvement of the health of the community it serves
   C. courteous treatment of patients who are poor
   D. enforcement of the health laws of the city

   1.____

2. The MOST appropriate of the following statements for Miss Smith, who works in the cardiac clinic, to make when answering the clinic telephone is:

   A. This is the Cardiac Clinic. Who's calling please?
   B. Hello. This is Miss Smith.
   C. Cardiac Clinic, Miss Smith speaking. May I help you?
   D. Miss Smith speaking. To whom do you wish to speak?

   2.____

3. Of the following, the CHIEF reason why you should be familiar with medical terminology is so that you can

   A. be of greatest assistance to the doctors and nurses
   B. answer the patient's questions about their symptoms and treatments
   C. know what supplies to order for the clinic
   D. understand the medical publications which are sent to the clinic

   3.____

4. Assume that instructions have been issued in your clinic that medical information is not to be given to patients. Of the following, the BEST reason for this policy is that

   A. the relationship between the clinic staff and clinic patients, although friendly, should remain impersonal
   B. the health of a patient is a private matter which should not be discussed in public
   C. incorrect medical information might be given to the patient
   D. only the nurse in charge should be permitted to give medical information to patients

   4.____

5. Of the following, the BEST reason for keeping clinic records confidential is to

   A. protect the patient who may not want others to know certain information
   B. protect the health station in case errors have been made
   C. prevent publicity about the health station which may keep patients from coming to the clinics
   D. avoid the extra work involved in giving out information

   5.____

6. To give each patient who is to return to the clinic a card with the date of his next appointment written on it is

   6.____

A. unnecessary; it is sufficient to tell him when to come back
B. of little value; some of the patients may not be able to read English
C. impractical; too much time would be taken up in writing the cards
D. good practice; the patient would be less likely to forget his next date

7. When setting up a *tickler* file for patients' appointments in your clinic, you should arrange the cards according to the

   A. name of the patient
   B. date when the patient is due in the clinic
   C. condition for which the patient is being treated
   D. name of the doctor

8. Assume that you are responsible for maintaining the patients' record file in the clinic to which you are assigned. Frequently, the other clinics in the health center where you work borrow record cards from your clinic files.
The BEST way for you to avoid difficulty in locating cards which may have been borrowed by other clinics is to

   A. make out a duplicate card for any clinic that wishes to borrow a card from your file
   B. refuse to lend your card to any other clinic unless the other clinic's personnel officer promises to return the card in person
   C. report it to your supervisor if anyone fails to return a card after a reasonable time
   D. have the person who borrows a card fill out an out-of-file card and place it in the file whenever a record card is removed

9. Suppose that you are given an unalphabetized list of 500 clinic patients and a set of unalphabetized record cards. Your supervisor asks you to determine if there is a record card for each patient whose name is on the list.
For you to first arrange the record cards in alphabetical order before checking them with the names on the list is

   A. *desirable;* this will make it easier to check each name on the list against the patients' record cards
   B. *undesirable;* it is just as easy to alphabetize the names on the list as it is to rearrange the record cards
   C. *desirable;* this extra work with the record cards will give you more information about the patients
   D. *undesirable;* adding an extra step to the procedure makes the work too complicated

10. Suppose that you have been given about two thousand 3x5 cards to arrange in numerical order.
For you to sort the cards into broad groups, such as 1-100, 101-200, etc., and then arrange each group of cards in numerical order is

    A. *desirable;* you will not be so apt to lose your place if interrupted when working with small groups of cards
    B. *undesirable;* setting up a large number of groups of cards leads to more errors
    C. *desirable;* the work can be done more quickly and easily with smaller groups of cards than with the entire group at once
    D. *undesirable;* any procedure which requires so many steps wastes too much time

3 (#1)

11. Of the following, the MOST important reason for keeping accurate records of clinic patients is that

    A. these records provide valuable information for medical research purposes
    B. accurate records are necessary to provide satisfactory medical care for the patients on return visits
    C. complete records are necessary in order to prepare accurate and complete statistical reports on the work of the clinic
    D. these records will show the large amount of work performed in the clinic

12. Suppose that one of the doctors who has been seeing patients on Wednesday changes his clinic day to Thursday. Two women who have previously had Wednesday appointments ask to come in on Thursday because they have great confidence in this doctor.
    For you to try to make Thursday appointments for them would be

    A. *correct;* the wishes of the patients should be considered in making appointments
    B. *wrong;* if the request were granted, the other patients would also want to have their appointments changed
    C. *correct;* most patients would rather come to the clinic on Wednesdays
    D. *wrong;* patients should not become too dependent upon any one physician

13. Of the following, the CHIEF reason for paying attention to a complaint from a clinic patient is that

    A. government employees should always be courteous to the public
    B. most people like to have others pay attention to their complaints
    C. it does no harm to listen to complaints even if there is no merit to them
    D. the patient may have good reason to complain

14. Assume that it is the rule in the clinic that the doctor is to sign the personal record card of each patient he examines. While you are filing the patients' record cards after the doctor has left the clinic, you notice that he has not signed the card of one of the patients he examined. Of the following, the MOST appropriate action for you to take is to

    A. sign your own name on the card since the doctor has left the clinic
    B. write the doctor's name on the card and sign your initials
    C. file the unsigned card in the record file with the other cards
    D. hold the card out and return it to the doctor for his signature on his next visit

15. Assume that it is the rule in the clinic that no patient may be seen after 4:00 P.M. so that the physicians and nurses will have time to write up cases and prepare for the following day. A few minutes after 4:00 P.M., an old woman who says she is in great pain and discomfort appears and asks for a doctor.
    For you to try to arrange for a physician to see her is

    A. *proper;* other patients waiting in the clinic will see how kind you are to sick people
    B. *improper;* a rule should never be broken by public health personnel
    C. *proper;* rules should not be interpreted too strictly when dealing with sick people
    D. *improper;* the physician would be very annoyed if you disturbed him after 4:00 P.M.

16. Assume that you have been instructed to note on the record of each child who is vaccinated the lot number of the vaccine used.
    Of the following, the MOST probable reason for this instruction is so that

A. a record can be kept of how much vaccine is used every year
B. if the child has an unfavorable reaction, the lot may be tested to determine the reason
C. no child will receive more than one vaccination
D. the oldest vaccine will be used first

17. The mother of a young child who is to be vaccinated against smallpox informs you that he gets hysterical at the sight of a needle.
Of the following, the BEST thing for you to do is to

    A. assure the mother that the child's fears are groundless
    B. speak to the child about the need to be protected against a serious disease like smallpox
    C. tell the head nurse about the child's fear before he is called for vaccination
    D. promise the child a lollypop or toy if he behaves and does not cry

18. A 10-year-old boy who is grossly overweight refuses to remove any of his clothing before being weighed, apparently because of embarrassment.
Of the following, it is BEST for you to

    A. weigh him fully dressed and note this fact on the record
    B. insist that he remove his clothing since otherwise the record would be inaccurate
    C. note on the record card *grossly overweight,* as you cannot weigh him with his clothing
    D. ask the head nurse to use her authority to make the boy undress

19. You notice that an 8-year-old boy who attends the clinic stammers badly.
Of the following, it is BEST for you to

    A. tell the doctor about his stammering in the boy's presence
    B. tell the boy each time you see him that his speech has improved
    C. ask the boy if he would like to go to a speech correction clinic
    D. make no reference to his stammer in the boy's presence

20. Of the following, the MOST important reason why you should remain with a 4-year-old child when his temperature is being taken by mouth is that otherwise the child might

    A. fall off the chair and fracture an arm or leg
    B. break the thermometer while it is in his mouth
    C. remove the thermometer from his mouth and misplace it
    D. leave the examining room and return to his mother

21. The BEST way to take the temperature of an infant is by

    A. feeling his forehead
    B. using an oral thermometer
    C. placing a thermometer under his armpit
    D. using a rectal thermometer

22. When the temperature of an adult is taken rectally, it is LEAST accurate to say that the

    A. temperature reading will be higher than if it were taken orally
    B. thermometer should be lubricated before use

C. thermometer should be in place for at least ten minutes
D. temperature reading is likely to be more accurate than if it were taken orally

23. When the temperature of an adult is taken orally, it is LEAST accurate to say that the

   A. thermometer should be washed with alcohol before it is used
   B. thermometer should be taken down below 96° F before it is used
   C. patient's temperature may be taken immediately after he has smoked a cigarette
   D. patient should be inactive just before his temperature is taken

24. The nurse described the test to the patient before bringing him to the examining room for a basal metabolism test.
    Her action may BEST be described as

   A. *correat;* the patient will be more cooperative if he knows what to expect
   B. *wrong;* the nurse does not know how the test will affect the patient
   C. *correct;* the nurse can judge whether the patient is too upset by this information to take the test
   D. *wrong;* explaining the test beforehand will only make the patient nervous

25. When a patient's sputum test is *positive,* it means that the

   A. patient's sputum is plentiful
   B. doctor has made an accurate diagnosis
   C. patient has recovered and is now in good health
   D. laboratory reports that the patient's sputum contains certain disease germs

26. A biopsy can BEST be described as a(n)

   A. pre-cancerous condition   B. examination of tissues
   C. living organism   D. germicidal solution

27. The *scratch* or *patch* test is usually given when testing for

   A. allergies   B. rheumatic fever
   C. blood poisoning   D. diabetes

28. Gamma globulin is frequently given to children after exposure to and before the appearance of symptoms of

   A. measles   B. smallpox
   C. tetanus   D. chickenpox

29. Of the following, the one which is NOT a respiratory disease is

   A. bronchitis   B. pneumonia
   C. nephritis   D. croup

30. A physician who specializes in the treatment of conditions affecting the skin is known as a

   A. urologist   B. dermatologist
   C. toxicologist   D. ophthalmologist

31. The branch of medicine which deals with diseases peculiar to women is

    A. pathology   B. orthopedics
    C. neurology   D. gynecology

32. The branch of medicine which deals with diseases of old age is called

    A. pediatrics   B. geriatrics
    C. serology   D. histology

33. *Petit mal* is a form of

    A. epilepsy   B. syphilis
    C. diabetes   D. malaria

34. Glaucoma is a disease of the

    A. thyroid gland   B. liver
    C. bladder   D. eye

35. A patient who has edema has

    A. not enough red blood cells
    B. too much water in the body tissues
    C. blood in the urine
    D. a swollen gland

36. The thoracic area of the body is located in the

    A. abdomen   B. lower back
    C. chest   D. neck

37. An electrocardiograph is MOST usually used in examination of the

    A. brain   B. heart
    C. kidney   D. gall bladder

38. The word *coagulate* means MOST NEARLY to

    A. bleed excessively   B. break up
    C. work together   D. form a clot

39. A stethoscope is used to examine the patient's

    A. heart   B. patellar reflex
    C. blood cells   D. spinal fluid

40. A pelvimeter is MOST usually used in the examination of a patient in the _____ clinic.

    A. chest   B. cancer   C. prenatal   D. eye

41. Tuberculin may BEST be described as a

    A. virus infection of the lungs
    B. preparation used in the diagnosis of tuberculosis
    C. sanitarium for tuberculous patients
    D. form of cancer of the lung

42. An autoclave is a(n)

    A. automatic dispenser of instruments needed for clinic examinations
    B. sterile place for storing clinic supplies until they are needed
    C. apparatus for sterilizing equipment under steam pressure
    D. portable self-operating general anesthesia unit

43. Radiation therapy is

    A. the recording of electrical impulses of the body on a graph
    B. a study of the effects of radiation fall-out on the human body
    C. a form of treatment used for certain diseases
    D. the filming of internal parts of the body through the use of x-rays

44. Diathermy is the treatment of patients by

    A. scientific use of baths and mineral waters
    B. insertion of radium into diseased tissues
    C. intravenous feedings of vitamins and minerals
    D. electrical generation of heat in the body tissues

45. The measurement of blood pressure involves two readings, which are known as _____ and _____.

    A. metabolic; diastolic   B. systolic; diastolic
    C. metabolic; hyperbolic   D. hyperbolic; systolic

46. The Snellen chart is used in examinations of the

    A. eyes   B. blood   C. urine   D. bile

47. An enema is MOST generally used to

    A. induce vomiting   B. irrigate the stomach
    C. clear the bowels   D. drain the urinary bladder

48. A bronchoscope is usually used in examinations of the

    A. kidneys   B. heart   C. stomach   D. lungs

49. The Wassermann test is used to find out if a patient has

    A. diphtheria   B. leukemia
    C. scarlet fever   D. syphilis

50. If a boiling water sterilizer is used, the minimum time necessary to sterilize instruments is MOST NEARLY _____ hour(s).

    A. 1/2   B. 1   C. 1 1/2   D. 2

KEY (CORRECT ANSWERS)

1.	B	11.	B	21.	D	31.	D	41.	B
2.	C	12.	A	22.	C	32.	B	42.	C
3.	A	13.	D	23.	C	33.	A	43.	C
4.	C	14.	D	24.	A	34.	D	44.	D
5.	A	15.	C	25.	D	35.	B	45.	B
6.	D	16.	B	26.	B	36.	C	46.	A
7.	B	17.	C	27.	A	37.	B	47.	C
8.	D	18.	A	28.	A	38.	D	48.	D
9.	A	19.	D	29.	C	39.	A	49.	D
10.	C	20.	B	30.	B	40.	C	50.	A

TEST 2

DIRECTIONS: Each question or incomplete statement is followed by several suggested answers or completions. Select the one that BEST answers the question or completes the statement. *PRINT THE LETTER OF THE CORRECT ANSWER IN THE SPACE AT THE RIGHT.*

1. To sterilize towels and dry gauze dressings in the health clinic, it is MOST advisable to   1.____

    A. dip them in a sterilizing solution
    B. wash them with a strong detergent
    C. boil them in the sterilizer
    D. steam them under pressure

2. Sterilization by use of chemicals rather than by boiling water is indicated when the instrument   2.____

    A. is made of soft rubber
    B. has a sharp cutting edge
    C. has pus or blood on it
    D. was used more than 24 hours before sterilization

3. When dusting the furniture in the clinic, it is advisable to use a silicone-treated dustcloth CHIEFLY because the treated cloth will   3.____

    A. collect the dust more efficiently
    B. disinfect as well as dust the furniture
    C. not remove the wax from the furniture
    D. make it unnecessary to polish the furniture in the future

4. Assume that the clinic in which you work has issued instructions that all supplies containing poison are to have blue labels with the word *poison* clearly marked on the label, and that these supplies are to be kept in a storage cabinet separate from other supplies. You notice that a bottle with no label is on a shelf in the *poison* storage cabinet.
Of the following, the BEST action for you to take is to   4.____

    A. place the unlabeled bottle in the back of the regular storage cabinet
    B. put a blue label on the bottle and write *poison* on the label
    C. ask another public health employee to help you decide if the bottle contains poison
    D. pour the contents of the bottle into the slop sink and destroy the bottle

5. Assume that you have been assigned to care for the supply room, and have been instructed to use the items which have been in stock longest before using the newer stock. Of the following, the MOST practical and time-saving way to do this is to   5.____

    A. keep a record file of all supplies received and used
    B. write the dates when the supplies were received and used on the labels or containers
    C. place new supplies behind supplies of the same items already in stock
    D. keep the fastest moving stock in the most convenient places

43

6. The public health employee should know that clinic supplies should be reordered

   A. as soon as the last container of the item in the supply closet is used up
   B. in the same amount on the first working day of each month
   C. whenever a let-up in clinic work makes time available
   D. when the records show that the stock may possibly be depleted within a month

7. The CHIEF reason for storing x-ray film in lead containers is that lead containers protect the film from

   A. moisture in the atmosphere
   B. exposure to stray x-rays
   C. dust and other particles
   D. extreme changes in temperature

8. You have been instructed to keep all narcotics locked in a separate cabinet when storing supplies.
   The one of the following which should be kept locked in this cabinet is a preparation containing

   A. cortisone   B. codeine   C. caffeine   D. quinine

9. Of the following medical supplies, the one which should be refrigerated is

   A. vaseline jelly   B. paregoric
   C. aureomycin   D. aspirin tablets

10. The one of the following which is NOT an antiseptic or disinfectant is

    A. distilled water   B. alcohol
    C. lysol   D. hydrogen peroxide

11. The one of the following which is an anesthetic is

    A. novocaine   B. phenobarbital
    C. benzedrine   D. witch hazel

12. The wide use of antibiotics has presented a number of problems. Some patients become allergic to the drugs so that they cannot be used when they are needed. In other cases, after prolonged treatment with antibiotics, certain organisms no longer respond to them at all. This is one of the reasons for the constant search for more potent drugs.
    On the basis of this paragraph, the one of the following statements which is MOST NEARLY correct is that

    A. antibiotics have been used successfully for certain allergies
    B. antibiotics should never be used for prolonged treatment
    C. because they have developed an allergy to the drug, antibiotics cannot be used when needed for certain patients
    D. one of the reasons for the constant search for new antibiotics is that so many diseases have been successfully treated with these drugs

13. The over-use of antibiotics today represents a growing danger, according to many medical authorities. Patients everywhere, stimulated by reports of new wonder drugs, continue to ask their doctors for a shot to relieve a cold, grippe, or any of the other virus infections that occur during the course of a bad winter. But, for the common cold and many other virus infections, antibiotics have no effect.
On the basis of this paragraph, the one of the following statements which is MOST NEARLY correct is that

    A. the use of antibiotics is becoming a health hazard
    B. antibiotics are of no value in the treatment of many virus infections
    C. patients should ask their doctors for a shot of one of the new wonder drugs to relieve the symptoms of grippe
    D. the treatment of colds and other virus infections by antibiotics will lessen their severity

14. Statistics tell us that heart disease kills more people than any other illness, and the death rate still continues to rise. People over 30 have a fifty-fifty chance of escaping, for heart disease is chiefly an illness of people in late middle age and advanced years. Because there are more people in this age group living today than there were some years ago, heart disease is able to find more victims.
On the basis of this paragraph, the one of the following statements which is MOST NEARLY correct is that

    A. half of the people over 30 years of age have heart disease today
    B. more people die of heart disease than of all other diseases combined
    C. older people are the chief victims of heart disease
    D. the rising birth rate has increased the possibility that the average person will die of heart disease

15. There is evidence that some individuals, given three doses of polio vaccine, have not developed enough immunity to protect themselves against paralytic polio. It is thought that immunity will be increased by a fourth injection given no sooner than one year after the third injection and many health agencies have been giving a fourth injection to their patients.
On the basis of this paragraph, the one of the following statements which is MOST NEARLY correct is that

    A. three doses of polio vaccine will not give any protection from paralytic polio
    B. a fourth injection of polio vaccine guarantees immunity to polio
    C. the fourth injection of polio vaccine should be given as soon as possible after the third injection
    D. the fourth injection of polio vaccine should be given at least a year after the third injection

Questions 16-22.

DIRECTIONS: Questions 16 through 22 are to be answered on the basis of the following table.

REPORT ON PATIENTS ATTENDING SELECTED HEALTH CLINICS January to December (This Year)					
CLINICS	A	B	C	D	E
Child Health	62,400	70,200	81,900	83,400	22,300
Chest	53,300	52,000	64,800	47,600	4,500
Social Hygiene	24,500	21,900	18,400	13,500	4,100
Eye	10,600	12,600	13,300	13,800	4,200
Cardiac	1,400	1,600	1,700	1,300	400
Prenatal	1,300	1,800	1,700	1,800	500

16. On the basis of the above chart, the group with the LARGEST number of patients attending the eye clinics was

    A. B B. C C. A D. D

17. If the population of the area located around group E was 210,000, the percentage of this population who attended the eye clinic was MOST NEARLY

    A. .02% B. 2% C. 5% D. 21%

18. If the clinics were open 250 days, the average daily attendance at the social hygiene clinics in group C was MOST NEARLY

    A. 74 B. 88 C. 259 D. 736

19. The percentage of all patients attending group E clinics who attended the chest clinics was MOST NEARLY

    A. 5% B. 8% C. 13% D. 25%

20. If 25% of the patients attending prenatal clinics in group B also attended the cardiac clinics, the number of prenatal clinic patients in group B who did NOT attend the cardiac clinics was MOST NEARLY

    A. 400 B. 450 C. 1200 D. 1350

21. If the number of persons who attended all clinics in group A last year was 20% less than this year, the number who attended the group A clinics last year was MOST NEARLY

    A. 32,700 B. 130,800 C. 163,500 D. 196,200

22. Assume that at the end of the year it was found that half of the people who attended the group B chest clinics had been found to be free of disease, 1/3 were discharged as needing no further care, and the rest were instructed to return to the clinic for further treatment.
    The number of persons who were told to return for further treatment was MOST NEARLY

    A. 7,000 B. 14,000 C. 21,000 D. 35,000

Questions 23-34.

DIRECTIONS: Each of Questions 23 through 34 consists of a word, in capitals, followed by four suggested meanings of the word. For each question, indicate in the space at the right the letter preceding the word which means MOST NEARLY the same as the word in capitals.

23. PUNCTUAL

   A. usual B. hollow
   C. infrequent D. on time

24. BENEFICIAL

   A. popular B. forceful C. helpful D. necessary

25. TEMPORARY

   A. permanently B. for a limited time
   C. at the same time D. frequently

26. INQUIRE

   A. order B. agree C. ask D. discharge

27. SUFFICIENT

   A. enough B. inadequate
   C. thorough D. capable

28. AMBULATORY

   A. bedridden B. lefthanded
   C. walking D. laboratory

29. DILATE

   A. enlarge B. contract C. revise D. restrict

30. NUTRITIOUS

   A. protective B. healthful
   C. fattening D. nourishing

31. CONGENITAL

   A. with pleasure B. defective
   C. likeable D. existing from birth

32. ISOLATION

   A. sanitation B. quarantine
   C. rudeness D. exposure

33. SPASM

   A. splash B. twitch C. space D. blow

34. HEMORRHAGE

   A. bleeding B. ulcer
   C. hereditary disease D. lack of blood

Questions 35-40.

DIRECTIONS: Questions 35 through 40 are to be answered on the basis of the usual rules for alphabetical filing. For each question, indicate in the space at the right the letter preceding the name which should be filed THIRD in alphabetical order.

35. A. Hesselberg, Norman J.　　B. Hesselman, Nathan B.　　35._____
    C. Hazel, Robert S.　　　　　D. Heintz, August J.

36. A. Oshins, Jerome　　　　　　B. Ohsie, Marjorie　　　　　36._____
    C. O'Shaugn, F.J.　　　　　　D. O'Shea, Frances

37. A. Petrie, Joshua A.　　　　B. Pendleton, Oscar　　　　37._____
    C. Pertweee, Joshua　　　　　D. Perkins, Warren G.

38. A. Morganstern, Alfred　　　B. Morganstern, Albert　　 38._____
    C. Monroe, Mildred　　　　　 D. Modesti, Ernest

39. A. More, Stewart　　　　　　 B. Moorhead, Jay　　　　　 39._____
    C. Moore, Benjamin　　　　　 D. Moffat, Edith

40. A. Ramirez, Paul　　　　　　 B. Revere, Pauline　　　　 40._____
    C. Ramos, Felix　　　　　　　D. Ramazotti, Angelo

Questions 41-50.

DIRECTIONS: Questions 41 through 50 are to be answered on the basis of the usual rules of filing. Column I lists the names of 10 clinic patients. Column II lists the headings of file drawers into which you are to place the records of these patients. For each question, indicate in the space at the right the letter preceding the heading of the file drawer in which the record should be filed.

COLUMN I　　　　　　　　　　　　COLUMN II

41. Charles Coughlin　　　　　　A. Cab-Cep　　　　　　　　　41._____

42. Mary Carstairs　　　　　　　B. Ceq-Cho　　　　　　　　　42._____

43. Joseph Collin　　　　　　　 C. Chr-Coj　　　　　　　　　43._____

44. Thomas Chelsey　　　　　　　D. Cok-Czy　　　　　　　　　44._____

45. Cedric Chalmers　　　　　　　　　　　　　　　　　　　　　45._____

46. Mae Clarke　　　　　　　　　　　　　　　　　　　　　　　46._____

47. Dora Copperhead　　　　　　　　　　　　　　　　　　　　 47._____

48. Arnold Cohn　　　　　　　　　　　　　　　　　　　　　　 48._____

49. Charlotte Crumboldt　　　　　　　　　　　　　　　　　　 49._____

50. Frances Celine　　　　　　　　　　　　　　　　　　　　　50._____

KEY (CORRECT ANSWERS)

1. D	11. A	21. B	31. D	41. D
2. B	12. C	22. A	32. B	42. A
3. A	13. B	23. D	33. B	43. D
4. D	14. C	24. C	34. A	44. B
5. C	15. D	25. B	35. A	45. B
6. D	16. D	26. C	36. D	46. C
7. B	17. B	27. A	37. C	47. D
8. B	18. A	28. C	38. B	48. C
9. C	19. C	29. A	39. B	49. D
10. A	20. D	30. D	40. C	50. A

EXAMINATION SECTION
TEST 1

DIRECTIONS: Each question or incomplete statement is followed by several suggested answers or completions. Select the one that BEST answers the question or completes the statement. *PRINT THE LETTER OF THE CORRECT ANSWER IN THE SPACE AT THE RIGHT.*

1. Of the following, the MOST important reason for requiring that an employee have knowledge of medical office procedures is that   1.____

   A. she can take care of sick people in the absence of a doctor
   B. patients in the clinic will be impressed with her apparent knowledge
   C. she will be more helpful in her work at the clinic
   D. letters she may have to write will be more concise

2. A newly appointed employee should have a good understanding of her functions in the Department of Health.   2.____
   Of the following, the training which would be LEAST helpful to her in the performance of her functions is

   A. an understanding of the role of the Department of Health in the community
   B. development of skill in the technics of work in a health center
   C. information as to the services offered in the health center
   D. development of skill in the care of the sick in their own homes

3. If an employee were called upon at the same time to attend to each of the following, the one she should do FIRST is   3.____

   A. sterilize instruments used in the examination of the last patient
   B. answer the telephone
   C. give the patient who is just leaving another appointment
   D. check to see if a patient who has just arrived has an appointment

4. Of the following, the LEAST important reason for answering telephone calls promptly in the health clinic is that   4.____

   A. patients waiting in the clinic will be impressed with the self-importance of the employee
   B. patients calling for information will be answered quickly
   C. the public will get a favorable impression of the Department of Health
   D. it will result in better service by keeping the lines free for other calls

5. Assume that the physician assigned to the clinic in which you work calls the clinic and tells you that he has been detained for half an hour and will not be able to report at 1:00 P.M. as scheduled.   5.____
   You should

   A. not say anything about the call to anyone
   B. report this information to your immediate supervisor
   C. tell the patient scheduled for 1:00 P.M. to come back the next day
   D. tell the physician that he must come at 1:00 P.M. since a patient has been scheduled for that time

51

6. Assume that a physician who is examining a patient asks you to hand him a certain instrument from the tray. You do not know exactly what he is referring to.
The BEST thing for you to do is to

   A. give him an instrument which you think might be suitable for the examination
   B. ask him to repeat what he said
   C. admit that you cannot identify the instrument he wants
   D. tell him that there is no such instrument on the tray

7. Assume that a patient asks you to explain something the doctor told her about her illness which she says she does not understand.
For you to suggest that she tell the doctor that she did not understand what he told her and ask him to explain it again is

   A. *advisable;* the patient will be impressed by your interest in her
   B. *inadvisable;* patients get tired of the run-around
   C. *advisable;* the doctor is best qualified to answer questions concerning or affecting the patient's health
   D. *inadvisable;* the patient will lose confidence in your ability

8. Assume that, after you have been employed for several months, the nurse who is your immediate supervisor summons you to her office. She tells you that she has noticed on several occasions that you have been careless about your personal appearance. In this instance, it would be

   A. proper for you to tell her that your personal appearance is no concern of hers
   B. advisable for you to listen politely to her and then do nothing about it
   C. fitting for you to tell her that the other employees in the clinic are just as careless
   D. best for you to thank her for her interest and to tell her that you will make an effort to be more careful

9. One of the patients at the Health Center insists that she be sent to a different doctor as she does not like the doctor she saw last week.
Of the following answers, the one that is MOST advisable for you to give to the patient is that

   A. she will have to take whatever doctor is available
   B. all the clinic doctors are equally good
   C. you will try to send her to another doctor
   D. she should see the nurse in charge

10. Suppose that the doctor in the clinic has given you an order which is contrary to the usual clinic procedure. Of the following, the BEST action for you to take is to

    A. point out to the doctor the usual clinic procedure and then do as he tells you
    B. refuse to do what he tells you as it is contrary to the usual procedure
    C. refuse to do what he tells you and call the nurse in charge
    D. do as the doctor tells you and at the first opportunity report the occurrence to the nurse in charge

11. When filing some patients' record cards in an alphabetic file, you notice that one card obviously has been misfiled.
    In this case, it would be MOST advisable for you to

    A. pay no attention to this as you believe it was not your error
    B. pull out the card and file it correctly
    C. report this to the clinic supervisor and suggest to her that she reprimand the employee who you believe is responsible for the misfiling
    D. take no particular care in the future when filing cards since errors will occur anyway

12. Assume that you are working directly with children in a well baby clinic. You feel feverish.
    Of the following, the BEST action for you to take is to

    A. wait and see whether you feel better; you don't want to seem to be a chronic complainer
    B. report immediately to the nurse in charge that you do not feel well
    C. take your temperature and, if it is over 101° F, report to the nurse in charge
    D. report to the nurse in charge only if you have other symptoms

13. As a receptionist in a public health center, you have certain responsibilities towards patients and other callers. You should greet each caller promptly and courteously. Never keep a caller waiting while you carry on a personal conversation, either on the telephone or with another employee. However, if you are occupied with clinic matters, give the caller to understand that you will be with him in a short while.
    On the basis of this paragraph, if a caller comes in while you are discussing with the nurse in charge coverage of the clinic during the lunch hour, the one of the following actions which would be the BEST for you to take is to

    A. stop and take care of his needs immediately as you should never keep a caller waiting
    B. nod to him and continue making plans for clinic coverage
    C. say to him that you will take care of him in a moment; then finish making your plans for clinic coverage
    D. finish making plans for clinic coverage with the nurse in charge and then inquire into the caller's needs

14. Assume that you are responsible for scheduling clinic appointments. One of the patients who has to report to the clinic every Tuesday morning asks that his appointments be scheduled for the last half hour of the clinic session. It has been the practice in this clinic to keep the last half hour open only for emergency appointments, and to schedule all appointments in order, from the time when the clinic opens.
    Of the following, the BEST action for you to take is to

    A. schedule the appointment at the time requested by the patient as he probably has a good reason for wanting it then
    B. disregard his request as no one attending a clinic should be given special consideration
    C. deny his request unless he has a medical reason for asking for a late appointment
    D. refer the request to the nurse in charge to determine if he should be given a late appointment

15. Suppose that a patient who is registered in the Social Hygiene Clinic of a Health Center appears in a drunken condition for a scheduled appointment.
Of the following, the BEST action for you to take is to

    A. inform the nurse in charge of the situation
    B. have him await his turn with the other patients
    C. send him home, telling him not to return until he is sober
    D. arrange for him to see the doctor immediately

16. Assume that you have been asked by your supervisor to instruct a newly-appointed aide in the performance of a given task.
Of the following, the BEST procedure for you to follow is

    A. to check her work only once after you have shown her how to do it; continued supervision after this should be the supervisor's responsibility
    B. not to check her work after you have shown her how to do it as she may resent your supervision
    C. not to check her work immediately but wait until she has done the task several times in order to give her a fair chance
    D. to check her work at frequent intervals after you have shown her how to do it until she is able to perform the given task

17. A worker should be carefully introduced to the clinic to which she has been assigned. The period of orientation will vary widely with the individual, her previous experience, and the type of clinic to which she is assigned.
In general, it will include an introduction to the physical set-up, the personnel, the type of service to be rendered, and the ideals of the clinic. In the beginning, the new worker should be given simple assignments and close supervision. The program should be arranged so as to give the nurse in charge opportunity to study the worker as to personality, general ability, or any special handicaps.
According to this paragraph, the one of the following statements that is MOST accurate is that, during the first few days, the new worker should

    A. do nothing but observe the physical set-up, the personnel, the type of service rendered, the ideals of the clinic
    B. be given a 30 hour course in the clinic to which she is assigned, including the physical set-up, the personnel, the ideals of the clinic
    C. be observed by the nurse in charge as to her ability to do the work in the clinic to which she has been assigned
    D. be closely supervised by the nurse in charge until she has a thorough knowledge of the clinic

18. Preparing a patient for physical examination has important mental aspects. Because each patient is individual in his reactions, a worker must plan her approach so as to deal with these reactions sympathetically. Thus, one patient may be afraid of the pain an examination may cause him immediately, another may fear that he will have unpleasant effects later, and still another may be only curious about the examination and have neither fear nor anxiety.
On the basis of this paragraph, the one of the following statements that BEST describes the reactions of patients when undergoing examination is that all patients

    A. are afraid when being examined
    B. react differently to an examination
    C. are afraid of the after-effects of an examination
    D. are curious about the examination

19. A recently published article states: Weight for height and age is, as many have previously held, an inadequate index of the *nutritional status* of a child. It is unscientific and unfair to set average weight as a goal for all children or for an individual child. Weighing and measuring, however, should be continued as a record of the trend of individual growth which is of value to the physician in relation to other findings and as valuable devices to interest the child in his growth.
    According to this article, weighing and measuring the height of children

    A. are of no value and should be stopped
    B. are useful to the physician
    C. are of no value but give interesting information
    D. indicate the nutritional status of the child

20. Blood pressure is the force that the blood exerts against the walls of the vessels through which it flows. The blood pressure is commonly meant to be the pressure in the arteries. The pressure in the arteries varies with the contraction (work period) and the relaxation (rest period) of the heart. When the heart contracts, the blood in the arteries is at its greatest pressure. This is called the systolic pressure. When the heart relaxes, the blood in the arteries is at its lowest pressure. This is called the diastolic pressure. The difference between both pressures is called the pulse pressure.
    The one of the following statements that is MOST accurate on the basis of this paragraph is that

    A. the blood in the arteries is at its greatest pressure during contraction
    B. systolic pressure measures the blood in the arteries when the heart is relaxed
    C. blood pressure is determined by obtaining the difference between systolic and diastolic pressure
    D. pulse pressure is the same as blood pressure

21. Lymph is a clear fluid, rich in white blood cells, and is actually blood plasma which has filtered through the walls of capillaries. It is circulated through the lymph vessels and in all the tissue spaces of the body. It carries nourishment and oxygen to the tissues and waste products away from them.
    The one of the following statements that is NOT correct on the basis of this paragraph is that lymph

    A. contains red blood cells
    B. contains white blood cells
    C. is a basic part of blood
    D. is circulated through the body

22. When storing medical supplies, it is important to remember that liquids should be labeled

    A. only if the liquids are poisonous and there is the slightest chance that they will not be recognized
    B. whenever there is the slightest chance that they will not be recognized
    C. at all times, and discarded if labels have become detached
    D. only in those cases where the liquids will be given to patients

23. When dusting metal countertops in the clinic, it is BEST to use a clean cloth which is

    A. medicated   B. wet   C. dry   D. damp

24. Of the following statements concerning a hypodermic syringe, the one that is MOST correct is that a plunger

    A. used for taking blood specimens can be used with any syringe barrel
    B. can be used for any syringe barrel as long as it goes in easily
    C. can be used only with the syringe barrel that was made for it
    D. must be used with the syringe barrel that was made for it only if it is to be used for injections

24.____

25. The one of the following which should NOT be done when using a thermometer is to

    A. shake down the thermometer to 95F before taking the patient's temperature
    B. ask the patient to keep his lips closed when taking the temperature orally
    C. wash the thermometer in hot soapy water after use
    D. keep the thermometer in a container of alcohol when not in use

25.____

26. The temperature of an adult when taken by rectum is usually _____ than if taken _____ under the armpit.

    A. *higher;* either by mouth or
    B. *higher;* by mouth and lower than if taken
    C. *lower;* either by mouth or
    D. *lower;* by mouth and higher if taken

26.____

27. Of the following tests, the one which is associated with tuberculosis is the _____ test.

    A. Schick   B. Mantoux   C. Dick   D. Kahn

27.____

28. A needle that has been used to draw blood should be rinsed immediately after use in

    A. a disinfectant solution   B. hot water
    C. cold water   D. hot, soapy water

28.____

29. Of the following, the statement that is MOST correct is that a hypodermic needle should be checked for burrs, hooks, and sharpness

    A. once a week
    B. before it is sterilized
    C. after it has been sterilized
    D. after it has been used three or four times

29.____

30. The MOST accurate of the following statements is that, when a syringe and needle are being sterilized by boiling, the

    A. plunger must be completely out of the barrel
    B. needle should be left attached to the barrel as when in use
    C. plunger may be completely inside the barrel
    D. needle should be boiled at least twice as long as the syringe

30.____

31. Of the following, the MOST important reason for washing an instrument in hot soapy water is to

    A. sterilize the instrument
    B. destroy germs by heat
    C. destroy germs by coagulation
    D. remove foreign matter and bacteria

31.____

32. Assume that a hypodermic needle which is to be used for injection is accidentally brushed at the tip by your hand. Of the following, the action which should be taken before this needle is used is that it be

    A. washed under the hot water tap
    B. wiped with a sterile piece of gauze
    C. washed in hot soapy water, then rinsed in sterile water
    D. boiled for ten minutes

33. The CORRECT way to sterilize a scalpel is to

    A. place it in a chemical germicide
    B. boil it for 10 minutes
    C. put it in the autoclave
    D. pass it through a bright flame

34. Assume that a tray of instruments has been accidentally left uncovered for five minutes after it had been sterilized.
    Of the following, the action you should take to ensure that the instruments are sterile for use is to

    A. dip them in boiling water
    B. boil them for 10 minutes
    C. replace the cover on the tray
    D. wipe each instrument with sterile gauze

35. An intramuscular injection is MOST likely to be used in the administration of

    A. smallpox vaccine   B. streptomycin
    C. glucose   D. blood

36. The one of the following which is NOT a normal element of blood is

    A. hemoglobin   B. a leucocyte
    C. marrow   D. a platelet

37. Of the following statements regarding the Salk vaccine, the MOST accurate one is that it

    A. immunizes children and adults against paralytic poliomyelitis
    B. is a test to determine the presence of poliomyelitis virus in the blood
    C. is a test to determine whether a child is immune to poliomyelitis
    D. is used in the treatment of patients suffering from paralytic poliomyelitis

38. The GREATEST success in the treatment of cancer has been in cancer of the

    A. blood   B. stomach   C. liver   D. skin

39. An autopsy is a(n)

    A. type of blood test
    B. examination of tissue removed from a living organism
    C. examination of a human body after death
    D. test to determine the acidity of body fluids

40. The word *vascular* is MOST closely associated with

   A. the circulatory system
   B. respiration
   C. digestion
   D. the nervous system

41. The word *diagnosis* means MOST NEARLY

   A. preparation of a diagram
   B. determination of an illness
   C. medical examination of a patient
   D. written prescription

42. A tendon connects

   A. bone to bone
   B. muscle to bone
   C. muscle to muscle
   D. muscle to ligament

43. Blood takes on oxygen as it passes through the

   A. liver   B. heart   C. spleen   D. lungs

44. The fatty substance in the blood which is deposited in the artery walls and which is believed to cause hardening of the arteries is called

   A. amino acid   B. phenol   C. cholesterol   D. pectin

45. The digestive canal includes the

   A. stomach, small intestine, large intestine, and rectum
   B. stomach, larynx, large intestine, and rectum
   C. trachea, small intestine, large intestine, and rectum
   D. stomach, small intestine, large intestine, and abdominal cavity

46. When giving artificial respiration, it should be kept in mind that air is drawn into the lungs by the

   A. expansion of the chest cavity
   B. contraction of the chest cavity
   C. expansion of the lungs
   D. contraction of the lungs

47. The formula for converting degrees Centigrade to degrees Fahrenheit is as follows:

   Fahrenheit = 9/5 of Centigrade + 32°, or
   (multiply the number of degrees Centigrade by 9, divide by 5 and add 32)

   If the Centigrade thermometer reads 25°, the temperature, in degrees Fahrenheit, is

   A. 13   B. 45   C. 53   D. 77

48. To make a certain preparation, you have been told to mix one ounce of Liquid A and 3 ounces of Liquid B.
    If you have used 18 ounces of Liquid B in preparing a larger amount, the number of ounces of Liquid A you should use is

    A. 6   B. 15   C. 21   D. 54

49. If one inch is equal to approximately 2.5 centimeters, the number of inches in fifteen centimeters is MOST NEARLY

    A. 1.6   B. 6   C. 12.5   D. 37.5

Questions 50-52.

DIRECTIONS: Questions 50 through 52 are to be answered on the basis of the following situation.

you have been asked to keep records of the time spent with each patient by the doctors in the clinic where you are assigned, Iour notes show that Dr. Jones spent the following amount of time with each patient he examined on a certain day:

    Patient A - 14 minutes;   Patient B - 13 minutes;
    Patient C - 34 minutes;   Patient D - 48 minutes;
    Patient E - 26 minutes;   Patient F - 20 minutes;
    Patient G - 25 minutes.

50. The average number of minutes spent by Dr. Jones with each patient is MOST NEARLY

    A. 20   B. 25   C. 30   D. 35

51. If Dr. Jones is to take care of the seven patients mentioned above at one session, the number of hours he will have to remain at the clinic is MOST NEARLY _____ hour(s).

    A. 1   B. 2   C. 3   D. 4

52. The one of the following groups of patients that required the LEAST time to be examined is Patients

    A. A, C, and E   B. B, D, and F
    C. C, E, and G   D. A, D, and G

Questions 53-60.

DIRECTIONS: Questions 53 through 60 are to be answered on the basis of the usual rules of filing. Column I lists the names of 8 clinic patients. Column II lists the headings of file drawers into which you are to place the records of these patients. In the space at the right, corresponding to the names in Column I, print the letter preceding the heading of the file drawer in which the record should be filed.

COLUMN I

53. Thomas Adams
54. Joseph Albert
55. Frank Anaster
56. Charles Abt
57. John Alfred
58. Louis Aron
59. Francis Amos
60. William Adler

COLUMN II

A. Aab-Abi
B. Abj-Ach
C. Aci-Aco
D. Acp-Ada
E. Adb-Afr
F. Afs-Ago
G. Agp-Ahz
H. Aia-Ako
I. Akp-Ald
J. Ale-Amo
K. Amp-Aor
L. Aos-Apr
M. Aps-Asi
N. Asj-Ati
O. Atj-Awz

53.____
54.____
55.____
56.____
57.____
58.____
59.____
60.____

KEY (CORRECT ANSWERS)

1. C	16. D	31. D	46. A
2. D	17. C	32. D	47. D
3. B	18. B	33. A	48. A
4. A	19. B	34. B	49. B
5. B	20. A	35. B	50. B
6. C	21. A	36. C	51. C
7. C	22. C	37. A	52. A
8. D	23. D	38. D	53. D
9. D	24. C	39. C	54. I
10. A	25. C	40. A	55. K
11. B	26. A	41. B	56. B
12. B	27. B	42. B	57. J
13. C	28. C	43. D	58. M
14. D	29. B	44. C	59. J
15. A	30. A	45. A	60. E

TEST 2

DIRECTIONS: Each question or incomplete statement is followed by several suggested answers or completions. Select the one that BEST answers the question or completes the statement. *PRINT THE LETTER OF THE CORRECT ANSWER IN THE SPACE AT THE RIGHT.*

Questions 1-6.

DIRECTIONS: In answering Questions 1 through 6, alphabetize the four names listed in each question; then print in the space at the right the four letters preceding the alphabetized names to show the CORRECT alphabetical arrangement of the four names.

1. A. Frank Adam   B. Frank Aarons   1.____
   C. Frank Aaron   D. Frank Adams

2. A. Richard Lavine   B. Richard Levine   2.____
   C. Edward Lawrence   D. Edward Loraine

3. A. G. Frank Adam   B. Frank Adam   3.____
   C. Fanny Adam   D. Franklin Adam

4. A. George Cohn   B. Richard Cohen   4.____
   C. Thomas Cohane   D. George Cohan

5. A. Paul Shultz   B. Robert Schmid   5.____
   C. Joseph Schwartz   D. Edward Schmidt

6. A. Peter Consilazio   B. Frank Consolezio   6.____
   C. Robert Consalizio   D. Ella Consolizio

Questions 7-13.

DIRECTIONS: For Questions 7 through 13, select the letter preceding the word which means MOST NEARLY the same as the word in capital letters.

7. LEGIBLE   7.____
   A. readable   B. eligible   C. learned   D. lawful

8. OBSERVE   8.____
   A. assist   B. watch   C. correct   D. oppose

9. HABITUAL   9.____
   A. punctual   B. occasional
   C. usual   D. actual

10. CHRONOLOGICAL   10.____
    A. successive   B. earlier
    C. later   D. studious

11. ARREST   11.____
    A. punish   B. run   C. threaten   D. stop

12. ABSTAIN   12.____
    A. refrain   B. indulge   C. discolor   D. spoil

13. TOXIC   13.____
    A. poisonous   B. decaying
    C. taxing   D. defective

14. TOLERATE   14.____
    A. fear   B. forgive   C. allow   D. despise

15. VENTILATE   15.____
    A. vacate   B. air   C. extricate   D. heat

16. SUPERIOR   16.____
    A. perfect   B. subordinate
    C. lower   D. higher

17. EXTREMITY   17.____
    A. extent   B. limb   C. illness   D. execution

18. DIVULGED   18.____
    A. unrefined   B. secreted
    C. revealed   D. divided

19. SIPHON   19.____
    A. drain   B. drink   C. compute   D. discard

20. EXPIRATION   20.____
    A. trip   B. demonstration
    C. examination   D. end

Questions 21-40.

DIRECTIONS: Column I lists 20 words, numbered 21 through 40, which are used in medical practice. Column II lists words or phrases which describe the words in Column I. In the space at the right, next to the number of each of the words in Column I, place the letter preceding the words or phrases in Column II which BEST describes the word in Column I.

COLUMN I

21. Anemia
22. Anesthetic
23. Arthritis
24. Aseptic
25. Astigmatism
26. Catheter
27. Cranium
28. Diathermy
29. Enema
30. Electrocardiograph
31. Forceps
32. Gynecology
33. Lesion
34. Lumbago
35. Microscope
36. Obstetrics
37. Ophthalmology
38. Postnatal
39. Rabies
40. Stethoscope

COLUMN II

A. A tube used to drain fluid from the bladder
B. The skull
C. Inflammation of a joint
D. A fluid injected into the rectum for the purpose of clearing out the bowels
E. A drug used in surgery which makes one insensible to pain
F. Rheumatic pain in the back
G. The branch of medicine concerned with diseases of the eye
H. Examination of the inner parts of the body by use of x-rays and a special screen
I. free from disease germs
J. Deficiency of blood
K. The branch of medicine concerned with diseases of women
L. A tumorous growth
M. A structural defect of the eye
N. An apparatus for sterilization under pressurized steam
O. The shoulder blade
P. A type of treatment which depends upon production of heat in the tissues by high frequency current
Q. An instrument for recording electric changes caused by contraction of the muscles of the heart
R. An instrument for magnifying minute organisms
S. The branch of medicine concerned with the care and delivery of pregnant women
T. A wound or injury
U. An acute infectious disease which is transmitted by the bite of dogs and other animals
V. A band of tissue which connects bones or holds organs in place
W. A medication used to calm nerves
X. An instrument used to listen to sounds in the heart
Y. A pair of tongs
Z. Occurring after birth

21. ____
22. ____
23. ____
24. ____
25. ____
26. ____
27. ____
28. ____
29. ____
30. ____
31. ____
32. ____
33. ____
34. ____
35. ____
36. ____
37. ____
38. ____
39. ____
40. ____

KEY (CORRECT ANSWERS)

1.	C,B,A,D	11.	D	21.	J	31.	Y
2.	A,C,B,D	12.	A	22.	E	32.	K
3.	C,B,D,A	13.	A	23.	C	33.	T
4.	D,C,B,A	14.	C	24.	I	34.	F
5.	B,D,C,A	15.	B	25.	M	35.	R
6.	C,A,B,D	16.	D	26.	A	36.	S
7.	A	17.	B	27.	B	37.	G
8.	B	18.	C	28.	P	38.	Z
9.	C	19.	A	29.	D	39.	U
10.	A	20.	D	30.	Q	40.	X

———

EXAMINATION SECTION
TEST 1

DIRECTIONS: Each question or incomplete statement is followed by several suggested answers or completions. Select the one that BEST answers the question or completes the statement. *PRINT THE LETTER OF THE CORRECT ANSWER IN THE SPACE AT THE RIGHT.*

1. The use of a solution of boiling water and bicarbonate of soda for sterilizing scalpels and other cutting instruments is

    A. *advisable;* all germs and bacteria will be efficiently removed from the instruments
    B. *inadvisable;* this process would dull the cutting edges of the instruments
    C. *advisable;* this procedure eliminates the necessity for washing soiled instruments
    D. *inadvisable;* boiling tends to rust these instruments

2. The autoclave is a(n)

    A. apparatus for sterilizing under pressure
    B. automatic stomach pump
    C. portable self-operating general anesthesia unit
    D. self-adjusting leg-splint

3. The MOST accurate of the following statements with regard to a patient's pulse is that

    A. the pulse should be taken by pressing the thumb against the artery on the wrist
    B. the pulse rate is not ordinarily affected by excitement or other emotional experiences
    C. the average normal pulse rate is 120-140 beats per minute
    D. in cases of severe shock, the pulse may become very rapid and weak

4. Incontinency is the term used to describe

    A. involuntary passage of urine
    B. nosebleed
    C. inflammation of a nerve
    D. a mild form of insanity

5. A biopsy is BEST described as a(n)

    A. post-mortem examination of a human body
    B. blood test
    C. examination of tissue removed from a living organism
    D. test to determine acidity of body fluids

6. Dyspepsia is BEST described as a condition in which there is

    A. great difficulty in breathing
    B. a disturbance of digestion
    C. lack of energy due to insufficient food
    D. an uncontrollable desire for alcoholic beverages

7. Hematology is the science concerned with the composition and function of

   A. blood
   B. bile
   C. spinal fluid
   D. gastric juice

8. The name of the test which is used to indicate immunity from or susceptibility to diphtheria is

   A. Snellen
   B. Dick
   C. Wassermann
   D. Schick

9. The one of the following which is a part of the nervous system is the

   A. spinal cord
   B. pancreas
   C. muscle
   D. cranium

10. Bacteria are known to flourish BEST in a place which is _____ and _____.

    A. cold; dry
    B. cold; damp
    C. hot; damp
    D. hot; dry

11. A mass program designed to curb the spread of poliomyelitis is based upon hypodermic injection of all children under 10 years of age with

    A. blood plasma
    B. cortisone
    C. ACTH
    D. gamma globulin

12. The one of the following which is a defect of vision is

    A. aphasia
    B. astigmatism
    C. caries
    D. toxemia

13. A band of fibrous connective tissue extending from a muscle to a bone is known as a

    A. tendon   B. vein   C. capillary   D. nerve

14. The biceps and triceps are the PRINCIPAL muscles of the

    A. leg   B. chest   C. neck   D. back

15. A cataract is a diseased condition of the

    A. brain   B. ear   C. eye   D. throat

16. The organ of the body which secretes bile is the

    A. stomach   B. liver   C. heart   D. kidney

17. Of the following, the one which is NOT a communicable disease is

    A. diabetes
    B. diphtheria
    C. smallpox
    D. typhoid fever

18. Of the following, the one which is NOT a part of the human skeleton is the

    A. femur   B. humerus   C. tibia   D. brain

19. An opinion as to the probable course and outcome of a disease is known as a(n)

   A. examination B. diagnosis
   C. case history D. prognosis

20. Argyrol is MOST commonly associated with treatment of the

   A. ear   B. eyes   C. mouth   D. nose

21. Of the following, the iron lung is MOST generally used in the treatment of

   A. heart disease B. rheumatic fever
   C. tuberculosis D. infantile paralysis

22. Post-partum care is GENERALLY given after

   A. a gall bladder operation
   B. shock therapy
   C. childbirth
   D. an x-ray examination

23. Of the following, the one which is NOT a method of x-ray examination is a

   A. pyelogram B. bronchogram
   C. G.I. series D. cardiogram

24. The basal metabolism test is used to

   A. determine the rate at which the body tissues are torn down and rebuilt while the patient is at complete rest
   B. study the vitamin and mineral needs of the body
   C. determine tendencies toward epileptic attacks under alternating conditions of stimulation and rest
   D. study the functioning of the heart at times of stress

25. When a person suffers a compound fracture of the leg, IN ALL PROBABILITY, the damaged bone is the

   A. radius or ulna B. clavicle
   C. sternum D. tibia or fibula

26. Fever, chills, inflamed eyelids, running nose, and cough are symptoms of

   A. measles B. chickenpox
   C. tuberculosis D. scarlet fever

Questions 27-38.

DIRECTIONS: Column I which follows lists 12 words, numbered 27 through 38, which are used in medical practice. Column II lists phrases which describe the words in Column I. In the space at the right, opposite the number preceding each of the words in Column I, place the letter preceding the phrase in Column II which BEST describes the word in Column I.

COLUMN I

27. Antidote
28. Asphyxiation
29. Cathartic
30. Congenital
31. Cyst
32. Fluoroscopy
33. Psychiatry
34. Pulmonary
35. Sedative
36. Subcutaneous
37. Transfusion
38. Vitamins

COLUMN II

A. Beneath the skin
B. Examination of the inner parts of the body by use of x-rays and a special screen
C. Relating to the lungs
D. The branch of medicine which specializes in diseases of the mind
E. An abnormal sac containing gas, fluid, or semi-solid matter
F. Medication to counteract poison
G. An instrument used to measure blood pressure
H. Loss of consciousness due to suffocation
I. Resistance to disease
J. Existing at birth
K. Medication used to quiet nerves
L. Abnormal bleeding
M. The transfer of blood from one person to another
N. Chemical substances, present in small amounts in various foods, which are essential to health
O. Purgative or laxative

27. _____
28. _____
29. _____
30. _____
31. _____
32. _____
33. _____
34. _____
35. _____
36. _____
37. _____
38. _____

Questions 39-50.

DIRECTIONS: Column I which follows lists 12 words, numbered 39 through 50, which are used in medical practice. Column II lists phrases which describe the words in Column I. In the space at the right, opposite the number preceding each of the words in Column I, place the letter preceding the phrase in Column II which BEST describes the word in Column I.

COLUMN I

39. Antiseptic
40. Cardiac
41. Epidermis
42. Glaucoma
43. Inoculation
44. Malignant growth
45. Obesity
46. Pediatrics
47. Respiration
48. Sputum
49. Tourniquet
50. Wassermann

COLUMN II

A. Expectorated matter, especially mucus
B. A branch of medicine which specializes in the treatment of children
C. Relating to the heart
D. Breathing
E. A substance which destroys disease germs
F. The outer layers of the skin
G. A disease of the eyeball
H. Inflammation of the mucous membrane
I. Overweight
J. Introduction of the virus of a particular disease into the system through the skin
K. A blood test for syphilis
L. An instrument used to stop the flow of blood from an artery due to an injury in the arm or leg
M. The collar bone
N. Cancerous tumor which resists treatment and tends to reappear after removal
O. Relating to the kidneys

39._____
40._____
41._____
42._____
43._____
44._____
45._____
46._____
47._____
48._____
49._____
50._____

KEY (CORRECT ANSWERS)

1. B	11. D	21. D	31. E	41. F
2. A	12. B	22. C	32. B	42. G
3. D	13. A	23. D	33. D	43. J
4. A	14. A	24. A	34. C	44. N
5. C	15. C	25. D	35. K	45. I
6. B	16. B	26. A	36. A	46. B
7. A	17. A	27. F	37. M	47. D
8. D	18. D	28. H	38. N	48. A
9. A	19. D	29. O	39. E	49. L
10. C	20. D	30. J	40. C	50. K

TEST 2

DIRECTIONS: Each question or incomplete statement is followed by several suggested answers or completions. Select the one that BEST answers the question or completes the statement. *PRINT THE LETTER OF THE CORRECT ANSWER IN THE SPACE AT THE RIGHT.*

1. Penicillin is effective in the treatment of several diseases because it   1._____

   A. builds up bodily resistance to the disease
   B. builds an immunity to the organisms causing the disease
   C. halts the growth of disease-producing organisms
   D. kills the organisms which cause the disease

2. The HIGHEST incidence of tuberculosis occurs during the ages of   2._____

   A. 1-9   B. 10-14   C. 15-30   D. 31-45

3. The MOST infectious stage of measles is the   3._____

   A. febrile   B. convalescent
   C. eruptive   D. coryzal

4. When caring for a child ill with measles, you should   4._____

   A. select a room which is light and airy, but you should protect the child's eyes from direct light
   B. regulate the temperature of the room to about 72-75° F
   C. keep the child in a darkened room to protect its eyes
   D. have the child wear woolen clothing for warmth

5. Ringworm on the skin is caused by a   5._____

   A. bacterium   B. fungus
   C. protozoan   D. worm

6. Body temperature taken by rectum is _____ body temperature taken orally.   6._____

   A. 1° lower than   B. the same as
   C. 1° higher than   D. 2° higher than

7. The dishes used by a patient ill with a communicable disease should be   7._____

   A. scraped and rinsed, then washed
   B. soaked overnight in a strong disinfectant solution
   C. boiled for twenty minutes
   D. kept separate and washed with soap and hot water

8. Cold applications tend to   8._____

   A. decrease the supply of blood in the area to which they are applied
   B. dilate the blood vessels
   C. bring a greater supply of blood to the area to which they are applied
   D. increase the pressure on the nerve endings

9. A bed cradle is a useful device for

   A. elevating an extremity
   B. keeping the weight of the upper bed covers off the patient
   C. helping to keep a restless patient in bed
   D. allowing for the free circulation of air

10. If a patient shows signs of a pressure sore at the base of the spine, the nurse should

    A. try a sitting position for the patient
    B. use small cotton rings on the pressure spot
    C. apply an ointment to the sore
    D. place an air-ring under the patient's buttocks

11. If a patient lying on her side is uncomfortable, the nurse may give her a(n)

    A. extra top cover
    B. back rest
    C. snug abdominal bandage
    D. pillow to support the lumbar region

12. The diet for a patient with gallstones may include

    A. grapefruit juice   B. liver
    C. cream   D. peas

13. A rich source of vitamin K is

    A. butter   B. spinach   C. oranges   D. milk

14. Flaxseed meal is prescribed for making an application of moist heat because of its

    A. medicinal properties   B. mucilaginous ingredients
    C. lightness   D. ability to retain heat

15. Of the following, the substance that is NOT commonly used as an emetic is

    A. bicarbonate of soda   B. mustard powder
    C. syrup of ipecac   D. table salt

16. Supervised practice periods are useful to

    A. insure continued practice on part of students
    B. prevent wrong bonds from becoming fixed through practice
    C. supplement class instruction
    D. teach children to study

17. The science of human behavior is called

    A. psychiatry   B. mental hygiene
    C. psychology   D. psychoanalysis

18. The microscopical examination of bacteria is used to determine

    A. best conditions for growth
    B. their virulency
    C. their size, shape, etc.
    D. their relation toward certain foods

19. A disease that confers active immunity is   19.____

    A. scarlet fever   B. erysipelas
    C. pneumonia   D. common colds

20. A serious infection of the eyes is   20.____

    A. trachoma   B. myopia
    C. astigmatism   D. amblyopia

21. A substance that inhibits the growth of bacteria but does NOT destroy them is called   21.____

    A. germicide   B. disinfectant
    C. antiseptic   D. sterilizer

22. Organisms which cause diseases of the intestinal tract are   22.____

    A. colon bacillus   B. diphtheria bacillus
    C. typhoid bacillus   D. cholera spirillum

23. Proved protection has been discovered against   23.____

    A. smallpox   B. mumps
    C. common colds   D. measles

24. Strabismus is commonly known as   24.____

    A. near-sightedness   B. far-sightedness
    C. cross-eyes   D. pink eyes

25. The country that has the HIGHEST death rate of mothers in childbirth is   25.____

    A. England   B. Italy
    C. China   D. United States

Questions 26-40.

DIRECTIONS: Complete the following statements.

26. A birth certificate may be obtained at the Bureau of _____.

27. The vitamin associated with pellagra is _____.

28. The source of insulin is _____.

29. Temporary teeth begin to appear about the age of _____.

30. Bovine tuberculosis affects _____.

31. Quarantine is _____.

32. At the end of the first year, a baby's weight should be _____.

33. An index of the cleanliness of a city's milk supply is determined by _____.

34. The antiscorbutic vitamin is _____.

35. Insulin was discovered by _____.

36. The vitamin associated with polyneuritis is _____.

37. The first permanent molar appears at the age of _____.

38. The separation of persons having communicable disease from others is known as _____.

39. The process of freeing matter from all germ life is _____.

40. Insulin shock is used in the treatment of _____.

Questions 41-50.

DIRECTIONS: Each question consists of a statement. You are to indicate whether the statement is TRUE (T) or FALSE (F).

41. Individuals can be tested for sensitivity to proteins before the injection of certain serums.

42. The optimum temperature of a schoolroom is 60-65° F.

43. Certified milk is the best grade of pasteurized milk.

44. Rickets in children is practically unknown today.

45. Children have a higher protein requirement proportionally than adults.

46. Stomatitis is an inflammation of the stomach.

47. A clean tooth never decays.

48. The enzyme in the digestive tract which aids in hydrolizing fats is steapsin.

49. All vegetables are good sources of proteins.

50. The commercial *diaper service* has proved itself safe and satisfactory.

KEY (CORRECT ANSWERS)

1. C
2. C
3. D
4. A
5. B
6. C
7. C
8. A
9. B
10. D
11. D
12. A
13. B
14. D
15. A
16. C
17. C
18. C
19. A
20. A
21. B
22. C
23. A
24. C
25. C
26. Records and Statistics, Health Department
27. B complex
28. pancreas
29. 7 months
30. cows (or milkers)
31. the enforced isolation of any person (or place) infected with a contagious disease and his contacts
32. 20 lbs.
33. bacterial counts
34. vitamin C
35. Drs. Banting, Best, and MacLeod in 1921
36. thiamin
37. 6 years
38. isolation
39. sterilization
40. manic depression
41. T
42. T
43. F
44. T
45. T
46. F
47. T
48. F
49. T
50. T

EXAMINATION SECTION
TEST 1

DIRECTIONS: Each question or incomplete statement is followed by several suggested answers or completions. Select the one that BEST answers the question or completes the statement. *PRINT THE LETTER OF THE CORRECT ANSWER IN THE SPACE AT THE RIGHT.*

1. The MOST common cause of death before age 65 is

    A. cerebrovascular disease
    B. malignant neoplasm
    C. heart disease
    D. diabetes mellitus
    E. liver cirrhosis

    1.____

2. Of the following, the disease NOT transmitted by mosquitoes is

    A. dengue fever
    B. lymphocytic choriomeningitis
    C. western equine encephalitis
    D. St. Louis encephalitis
    E. yellow fever

    2.____

3. The single MOST effective measure to prevent hookworm infection is

    A. washing hands
    B. washing clothes daily
    C. cooking food at high temperatures
    D. wearing shoes
    E. none of the above

    3.____

4. Transmission of tuberculosis in the United States occurs MOST often by

    A. fomites
    B. blood transfusion
    C. inhalation of droplet
    D. transplacentally
    E. milk

    4.____

5. The second MOST common cause of death in the United States is

    A. accident
    B. cancer
    C. cerebrovascular disease
    D. heart disease
    E. AIDS

    5.____

6. All of the following bacteria are spread through fecal-oral transmission EXCEPT

    A. haemophilus influenza type B
    B. campylobacter
    C. escherichia coli
    D. salmonella
    E. shigella

    6.____

7. Routine immunization is particularly important for children in day care because pre-school-aged children currently have the highest age specific incidence of all of the following EXCEPT

    A. H-influenzae type B
    B. neisseria meningitis
    C. measles
    D. rubella
    E. pertussis

    7.____

8. Hand washing and masks are necessary for physical contact with all of the following patients EXCEPT

   A. lassa fever
   B. diphtheria
   C. coxsackie virus disease
   D. varicella
   E. plaque

9. Control measures for prevention of tick-borne infections include all of the following EXCEPT:

   A. Tick-infested area should be avoided whenever possible.
   B. If a tick-infested area is entered, protective clothing that covers the arms, legs, and other exposed area should be worn.
   C. Tick/insect repellent should be applied to the skin.
   D. Ticks should be removed promptly.
   E. Daily inspection of pets and removal of ticks is not indicated.

10. The PRINCIPAL reservoir of giardia lamblia infection is

    A. humans
    B. mosquitoes
    C. rodents
    D. sandflies
    E. cats

11. Most community-wide epidemics of giardia lamblia infection result from

    A. inhalation of droplets
    B. eating infected meats
    C. eating contaminated eggs
    D. drinking contaminated water
    E. blood transfusions

12. Epidemics of giardia lamblia occurring in day care centers are USUALLY caused by

    A. inhalation of droplets
    B. person-to-person contact
    C. fecal and oral contact
    D. eating contaminated food
    E. all of the above

13. Measures of the proportion of the population exhibiting a phenomenon at a particular time is called the

    A. incidence
    B. prevalence
    C. prospective study
    D. cohort study
    E. all of the above

14. The occurrence of an event or characteristic over a period of time is called

    A. incidence
    B. prevalence
    C. specificity
    D. case control study
    E. cohort study

15. All of the following are live attenuated viral vaccines EXCEPT

    A. measles
    B. mumps
    C. rubella
    D. rabies
    E. yellow fever

16. Chlorinating air-cooling towers can prevent

    A. scarlet fever
    B. impetigo
    C. typhoid fever
    D. mycobacterium tuberculosis
    E. legionnaire's disease

17. Eliminating the disease causing agent may be done by all of the following methods EXCEPT

    A. chemotherapeutic
    B. cooling
    C. heating
    D. chlorinating
    E. disinfecting

18. Which of the following medications is used to eliminate pharyngeal carriage of neisseria meningitidis?

    A. Penicillin
    B. Rifampin
    C. Isoniazid
    D. Erythromycin
    E. Gentamicin

19. Post-exposure prophylaxis is recommended for rabies after the bite of all of the following animals EXCEPT

    A. chipmunks
    B. skunks
    C. raccoons
    D. bats
    E. foxes

20. To destroy the spores of clostridium botulinum, canning requires a temperature of AT LEAST _____ °C.

    A. 40   B. 60   C. 80   D. 100   E. 120

21. All of the following are killed or fractionated vaccines EXCEPT

    A. hepatitis B
    B. yellow fever
    C. H-influenza type B
    D. pneumococcus
    E. rabies

22. Of the following, the disease NOT spready by food is

    A. typhoid fever
    B. shigellosis
    C. typhus
    D. cholera
    E. legionellosis

23. In the United States, the HIGHEST attack rate of sheigella infection occurs in children between _____ of age.

    A. 1 to 6 months
    B. 6 months to 1 year
    C. 1 to 4 years
    D. 6 to 10 years
    E. 10 to 15 years

24. Risk factors for cholera include all of the following EXCEPT

    A. occupational exposure
    B. lower socioeconomic
    C. unsanitary condition
    D. high socioeconomic
    E. high population density in low income areas

25. The MOST common cause of traveler's diarrhea is 25.____

    A. escherichia coli   B. shigella
    C. salmonella   D. cholera
    E. campalobacter

KEY (CORRECT ANSWERS)

1.	C	11.	D
2.	B	12.	B
3.	D	13.	B
4.	C	14.	A
5.	B	15.	D
6.	A	16.	E
7.	B	17.	B
8.	C	18.	B
9.	E	19.	A
10.	A	20.	E

21.	B
22.	C
23.	C
24.	D
25.	A

TEST 2

DIRECTIONS: Each question or incomplete statement is followed by several suggested answers or completions. Select the one that BEST answers the question or completes the statement. *PRINT THE LETTER OF THE CORRECT ANSWER IN THE SPACE AT THE RIGHT.*

1. The increased prevalence of entamoeba histolytica infection results from   1.____

   A. lower socioeconomic status in endemic area
   B. institutionalized (especially mentally retarded) population
   C. immigrants from endemic area
   D. promiscuous homosexual men
   E. all of the above

2. The MOST common infection acquired in the hospital is _____ infection.   2.____

   A. surgical wound   B. lower respiratory tract
   C. urinary tract   D. bloodstream
   E. gastrointestinal

3. The etiologic agent of Rocky Mountain spotted fever is   3.____

   A. rickettsia prowazekii   B. rickettsia rickettsii
   C. rickettsia akari   D. coxiella burnetii
   E. rochalimaena quintana

4. The annual death rate for injuries per 100,000 in both sexes is HIGHEST in those _____ years of age.   4.____

   A. 1 to 10   B. 10 to 20   C. 30 to 40
   D. 50 to 60   E. 80 to 90

5. The death rate per 100,000 population due to motor vehicle accident is HIGHEST among   5.____

   A. whites   B. blacks
   C. Asians   D. native Americans
   E. Spanish surnamed

6. Among the following, the HIGHEST rate of homicide occurs in   6.____

   A. whites   B. blacks
   C. native Americans   D. Asians
   E. Spanish surnamed

7. All of the following are true statements regarding coronary heart disease EXCEPT: 7.____

   A. About 4.6 million Americans have coronary heart disease.
   B. Men have a greater risk of MI and sudden death.
   C. Women have a greater risk of angina pectoris.
   D. 25% of coronary heart disease death occurs in individuals under the age of 65 years.
   E. White women have a greater risk of MI and sudden death.

8. Major risk factors for coronary heart disease include all of the following EXCEPT

    A. smoking
    B. elevated blood pressure
    C. obesity
    D. high level of serum cholesterol
    E. family history of coronary heart disease

9. The MOST common cancer in American men is

    A. stomach   B. lung   C. leukemia
    D. prostate   E. skin

10. The HIGHEST incidence of prostate cancer occurs in _____ Americans.

    A. white   B. black   C. Chinese
    D. Asian   E. Spanish

11. All of the following are risk factors for cervical cancer EXCEPT

    A. smoking
    B. low socioeconomic condition
    C. first coital experience after age 20
    D. multiple sexual partners
    E. contracting a sexually transmitted disease

12. All of the following are independent adverse prognostic factors for lung cancer EXCEPT

    A. female sex
    B. short duration of symptom
    C. small cell histology
    D. metastatic disease at time of diagnosis
    E. persistently elevated CEA

13. Assuming vaccines with 80% efficacy were available in limited quantity, which vaccine among the following should be given to a military recruit?

    A. Polio   B. Pseudomonas
    C. Meningococcus   D. Influenza
    E. None of the above

14. Among the following, the vaccine which should be administered to children with sickle cell disease is

    A. influenza   B. meningococcus
    C. pseudomonas   D. pneumococcal
    E. yellow fever

15. All of the following are correct statements concerning gastric carcinoma in the United States EXCEPT:

    A. The risk for males is 2.2 times greater than for females.
    B. The incidence is increased.
    C. The risk is higher in persons with pernicious anemia than for the general population.

D. City dwellers have an increased risk of stomach cancer.
E. Workers with high levels of exposure to nickle and rubber are at increased risk.

16. During the first year of life, a condition that can be detected by screening is   16.____

    A. hypothyroidism
    B. RH incompatibility
    C. phenylketonuria
    D. congenital dislocation of the hip
    E. all of the above

17. The major reservoir of the spread of tuberculosis within a hospital is through   17.____

    A. patients   B. custodial staff
    C. doctors   D. nursing staff
    E. undiagnosed cases

18. All of the following statements are true regarding tuberculosis EXCEPT: 18.____

    A. Droplet nuclei are the major vehicle for the spread of tuberculosis infection.
    B. The highest incidence is among white Americans.
    C. There is a higher incidence of tuberculosis in prison than in the general population.
    D. HIV infection is a significant independent risk factor for the development of tuberculosis.
    E. A single tubercle bacillus, once having gained access to the terminal air spaces, could establish infection.

19. The human papiloma virus is associated with   19.____

    A. kaposi sarcoma
    B. hepatoma
    C. cervical neoplasia
    D. nasopharyngeal carcinoma
    E. none of the above

20. General recommendations for prevention of sexually transmitted diseases include all of   20.____
    the following EXCEPT

    A. contact tracing   B. disease reporting
    C. barrier methods   D. prophylactic antibiotic use
    E. patient education

21. Syphilis remains an important sexually transmitted disease because of all of the following   21.____
    EXCEPT its

    A. public health heritage
    B. effect on perinatal morbidity and mortality
    C. association with HIV transmission
    D. escalating rate among black teenagers
    E. inability to be prevented

22. Which of the following statements about homicide is NOT true? Approximately

    A. forty percent are committed by friends and acquaintances
    B. twenty percent is committed by spouse
    C. fifteen percent is committed by a member of the victim's family
    D. fifteen percent is committed by strangers
    E. fifteen percent are labeled *relationship unknown*

23. Conditions for which screening has proven cost-effective include

    A. phenylketonuria
    B. iron deficiency anemia
    C. lead poisoning
    D. tuberculosis
    E. all of the above

24. Suicide is MOST common among

    A. whites
    B. blacks
    C. hispanics
    D. Asians
    E. none of the above

25. The MOST frequenty used method of suicide is

    A. hanging
    B. poisoning by gases
    C. firearms
    D. drug overdose
    E. drowning

KEY (CORRECT ANSWERS)

1. E	11. C
2. C	12. A
3. B	13. C
4. E	14. D
5. D	15. B
6. B	16. E
7. E	17. E
8. C	18. B
9. D	19. C
10. B	20. D

21. E
22. B
23. E
24. A
25. C

EXAMINATION SECTION
TEST 1

DIRECTIONS: Each question or incomplete statement is followed by several suggested answers or completions. Select the one that BEST answers the question or completes the statement. *PRINT THE LETTER OF THE CORRECT ANSWER IN THE SPACE AT THE RIGHT.*

1. Dichloro-diphenyl-trichloroethane was used MOST effectively as a(n)
   A. disinfectant
   B. termite preventative
   C. moth preventative
   D. insecticide

   1.____

2. Learning by constant repetition without being aware of the thought behind what is being learned is
   A. book learning
   B. automation
   C. rationalization
   D. rote learning

   2.____

3. All of the following are common methods for treating drug addiction EXCEPT
   A. detoxification with guidance from healthcare professionals
   B. medication to manage cravings and withdrawal symptoms
   C. behavioral and psychological therapy
   D. institutionalization until the addiction is cured

   3.____

4. The purpose of vaccines is to
   A. reduce the causative organism
   B. develop scar tissue
   C. stimulate growth of antibodies
   D. produce bacteriostasis

   4.____

5. Of the following, the MOST dangerous narcotic is
   A. codeine
   B. opium
   C. heroin
   D. marijuana

   5.____

6. If a teenage girl is careless about putting her clothes away,
   A. put the clothing away for her
   B. tolerate the situation
   C. inspire her to be neat
   D. lecture her

   6.____

7. A two-year-old child that refuses to eat lunch should
   A. be forced to eat
   B. be appeased
   C. not be forced to eat, and the food should be removed without comment after a reasonable amount of time has passed
   D. be scolded

   7.____

8. Thumbsucking should be eliminated by
   A. satisfying the physical and emotional needs
   B. mechanical restraints
   C. applying distatseful compounds
   D. punishment

9. During the first three years, the strongest influence on the personality of a child is
   A. his or her friends
   B. the economic status of the family
   C. the social status of the family
   D. his or her relationships within the family

10. For 12-year-old children, an allowance
    A. may be used as a training device
    B. should be provided
    C. encourages a distorted sense of values
    D. provides a means of disciplinary control

11. When a 10-year-old boy temporarily becomes irritable and boisterous, parents should
    A. divert his attention
    B. punish him
    C. cater to his whims
    D. ascertain the reason

12. Parents should provide opportunities to habituate control of small muscles of the arms when the child
    A. eats solid food
    B. makes an effort to feed himself
    C. eats in restaurant
    D. attends school

13. Concerning a six-year-old child, parents who insist on absolute perfection may
    A. hamper future accomplishments
    B. encourage good habits
    C. increase mutual love
    D. destroy imitative performance

14. Lefthandedness
    A. is an individual trait
    B. should be corrected
    C. indicates a shortcoming
    D. is a conditioned reflex

15. To reduce fears in children, parents should
    A. give affection
    B. lecture them
    C. shield them
    D. provide safeguards

16. When a new baby is expected, to encourage a sense of belonging, older children should be allowed
    A. to anticipate another playmate
    B. no knowledge of the new baby
    C. to know, but not talk, about the new baby
    D. to share in the preparations

17. First-aid care of a third-degree burn requires 17.____
    A. oil and chalk mixture   B. sterile dressing
    C. antiseptic solution   D. healing ointment

18. Concerning teeth, 18.____
    A. dental caries appear most frequently between ages 12 and 20
    B. dental tartar should not be removed
    C. orthodontia is unimportant
    D. fluorides prevent all decay

19. Heat destroys bacteria by 19.____
    A. enucleation
    B. hemolysis
    C. coagulating protein
    D. making the cell wall permeable

20. The value of antihistaminic compounds lies PRIMARILY in their ability to 20.____
    A. increase intervals between infections
    B. relieve allergic manifestations
    C. immunize
    D. prevent the spread of infection

21. A test program that gives positive proof of drug addiction is through the use of 21.____
    A. hystidine   B. nalline   C. chlorine   D. choline

22. Drug withdrawal symptoms in addicts include vomiting and changes in 22.____
    A. muscular control   B. nerves
    C. color of the skin   D. pupils of the eyes

23. Overuse of NSAIDs like ibuprofen often leads to 23.____
    A. allergic reaction
    B. memory loss or dizziness
    C. sharp decrease in blood pressure
    D. gastrointestinal issues

24. Plantar fasciitis is a condition most likely to be diagnosed by a(n) 24.____
    A. dermatologist   B. hand specialist
    C. oncologist   D. podiatrist

25. Body Mass Index (BMI) is a numeric value used to classify patients as 25.____
    overweight or obese through the measurement of _____ and _____.
    A. height; weight   B. HDL; LDL
    C. pulse rate; breathing rate D. weight; cholesterol

26. The home can BEST benefit the mental health of its members through 26.____
    A. development of attitudes which result in appropriate emotional expression
    B. an elementary knowledge of psychiatry
    C. a check on the psychosomatics of the older members
    D. regular physical check-ups

27. When a child expresses fear of darkness on retiring, the BEST procedure is to 27._____
    A. make light of his fears
    B. compel him to accept the darkness
    C. provide a dim light
    D. shame him for his fears

28. Active immunity is acquired through 28._____
    A. production of antibodies
    B. imperviousness of skin tissue
    C. enzyme activity
    D. washing action of mucous membranes

29. The main criticism of body mass index as a measure of overall health is that it 29._____
    A. can cause mental health issues by classifying someone as obese
    B. fails to accurately account for muscle mass and body fat
    C. is too complex to provide an accurate assessment
    D. is too difficult to measure

30. A highly dangerous and addictive synthetic narcotic is 30._____
    A. amidol   B. amidone   C. cobalamine   D. pyridoxine

KEY (CORRECT ANSWERS)

1.	D	11.	D	21.	B
2.	D	12.	B	22.	D
3.	D	13.	A	23.	D
4.	C	14.	A	24.	D
5.	C	15.	A	25.	A
6.	C	16.	D	26.	A
7.	C	17.	B	27.	C
8.	A	18.	A	28.	A
9.	D	19.	C	29.	B
10.	A	20.	B	30.	B

TEST 2

DIRECTIONS: Each question or incomplete statement is followed by several suggested answers or completions. Select the one that BEST answers the question or completes the statement. *PRINT THE LETTER OF THE CORRECT ANSWER IN THE SPACE AT THE RIGHT.*

1. The Salk vaccine is administered to prevent
   A. measles
   B. diphtheria
   C. poliomyelitis
   D. whooping cough

2. Cancer of the blood is
   A. carcinoma
   B. sarcoma
   C. leukemia
   D. epithelioma

3. The accepted treatment in severe and extensive radiation burns is to FIRST
   A. apply tannic acid generously
   B. apply wet sodium bicarbonate dressing
   C. bandage the burned area firmly
   D. put the patient to bed

4. A bed cradle is a device for supporting the
   A. back
   B. knees
   C. bed covering
   D. food tray

5. Pediculosis Capitus refers to
   A. baldness
   B. athlete's foot
   C. lice
   D. tics

6. The MAIN purpose of a good nursing chart is to
   A. aid the nurse's memory
   B. help the doctor in diagnosis and treatment
   C. prevent lawsuits
   D. protect the hospital

7. When an ice bag is applied, it should be
   A. kept filled with ice
   B. strapped in place
   C. removed every 15 or 20 minutes
   D. removed every hour

8. Hepatitis is a disease of the
   A. renals
   B. spleen
   C. liver
   D. pancreas

9. Bones are joined to one another with
   A. sinews
   B. tendons
   C. ligaments
   D. membranes

10. Average adult pulse rate for a man is
    A. 64 B. 72 C. 80 D. 96

11. In MOST cases, to get a doctor in an emergency, call the
    A. nearest doctor
    B. nearest hospital
    C. Red Cross
    D. police emergency 911

12. Intravenous injections may be legally administered by the
    A. registered nurse
    B. practical nurse
    C. nursing aide
    D. home nurse

13. Persons who are likely to come in contact with communicable diseases are immunized by
    A. heredity
    B. environment
    C. asepsis
    D. biotics

14. The temperature of water for a hot water bottle should NOT exceed
    A. 100°F B. 150°F C. 125°F D. 175°F

15. The currently accepted treatment for arthritis is
    A. x-ray
    B. cortisone
    C. aureomycin
    D. gold injections

16. The MOST reliable temperature is that found in the
    A. rectum
    B. axilla
    C. mouth
    D. none of the above

17. An antiseptic solution recommended in first aid for slight skin scratches (abrasions) is
    A. concentrated boric acid
    B. tincture of merthiolate 1:1000
    C. iodine 2%
    D. tincture of green soap

18. The MOST frequent cause of death in the United States today is
    A. cancer
    B. tuberculosis
    C. Alzheimer's disease
    D. heart disease

19. Average adult temperature by rectum is ____°F.
    A. 99.6 B. 97.6 C. 98.6 D. 100.6

20. Metaplasia refers to disturbances of the
    A. mucous membranes
    B. epithelial tissues
    C. cartilage
    D. basal metabolism

21. A subjective symptom is one that the patient
    A. feels
    B. hears
    C. sees
    D. smells

22. A bed cradle
    A. keeps the patient's weight off the bed
    B. keeps the knees up
    C. elevates the feet
    D. keeps the weight of the covers off the patient

23. Statistics indicate that MOST youths start the drug habit with
    A. marijuana   B. heroin   C. cocaine   D. morphine

24. A stroke may be caused by
    A. cerebral hemorrhage   B. caecal dilation
    C. aortal thrombosis   D. pleural edema

25. The control of automatic breathing is located in the
    A. cerebrum   B. cerebellum
    C. spinal cord   D. medulla oblongata

26. The water for a baby's bath should be closest to ____°F.
    A. 80   B. 90   C. 100   D. 110

27. The Schick test indicates immunity to
    A. diphtheria   B. smallpox   C. tetanus   D. tuberculosis

28. Difficulty in speaking is known as
    A. asphyxia   B. aphasia   C. amnesia   D. anorexia

29. A water blister should be
    A. opened and drained
    B. left unbroken
    C. painted with iodine and bandaged
    D. soaked in hot Epsom salt solution

30. The FIRST to be affected by the anesthetizing action of alcohol is the exercise of
    A. judgment   B. memory
    C. muscular coordination   D. control of speech

31. To the nervous system, alcohol acts as a
    A. depressant   B. stimulant   C. gratifier   D. agitator

32. Acute alcoholism may properly be labeled a psychosis because it involves
    A. intellectual limitations
    B. a loss of contact with reality
    C. emotional inadequacies
    D. bodily disease

33. Blood alcohol content is a measure of
    A. the amount of alcohol consumed in a 24-hour span
    B. the amount of alcohol in the blood
    C. the amount of alcohol it takes to intoxicate an average adult
    D. the effect of alcohol on blood thinning

34. Characteristic symptoms of chronic alcoholism include
    A. exiccosis
    B. damage to brain tissue
    C. increase in weight
    D. periods of depression

35. Alcohol is MOST often used excessively in order to
    A. induce sleep
    B. stimulate brain action
    C. overcome social inadequacy
    D. furnish temporary release from tensions

KEY (CORRECT ANSWERS)

1. C	11. D	21. A	31. A
2. C	12. A	22. D	32. B
3. C	13. D	23. A	33. B
4. C	14. C	24. A	34. D
5. C	15. B	25. D	35. D
6. B	16. A	26. C	
7. C	17. C	27. A	
8. C	18. D	28. B	
9. C	19. C	29. B	
10. B	20. C	30. A	

EDUCATING AND INTERACTING WITH THE PUBLIC

These questions test for knowledge of techniques used to interact effectively with individual citizens and/or community groups, to educate or inform them about topics of concern, to publicize or clarify agency programs or policies, to negotiate conflicts or resolve complaints, and to represent one's agency or program in a manner in keeping with good public relations practices. Questions may also cover interacting with others in cooperative efforts of public outreach or service. There will be 15 questions in this subject area on the written test.

TEST TASK:
You will be presented with a variety of situations in which you must apply knowledge of how best to interact with other people.

SAMPLE QUESTION:
A person approaches you expressing anger about a recent action by your department. Which one of the following should be your first response to this person?

A. Interrupt to say you cannot discuss the situation until he calms down.
B. Say you are sorry that he has been negatively affected by your department's action.
C. Listen and express understanding that he has been upset by your department's action.
D. Give him an explanation of the reasons for your department's action.

The correct answer to this sample question is choice C

C. SOLUTION:

Choice A *is not correct.* It would be inappropriate to interrupt. In addition, saying that you cannot discuss the situation until the person calms down will likely aggravate him further.

Choice B *is not correct.* Apologizing for your department's action implies that the action was improper.

Choice C is the correct answer to this question. By listening and expressing understanding that your department's action has upset him, you demonstrate that you have heard and understand his feelings and point of view.

Choice D *is not correct.* While an explanation of the reasons for the action may be appropriate at a later time, at this moment the person is angry and would not be receptive to such an explanation.

EXAMINATION SECTION
TEST 1

DIRECTIONS: Each question or incomplete statement is followed by several suggested answers or completions. Select the one that BEST answers the question or completes the statement. *PRINT THE LETTER OF THE CORRECT ANSWER IN THE SPACE AT THE RIGHT.*

1. When conducting a needs assessment for the purpose of education planning, an agency's FIRST step is to identify or provide
   A. a profile of population characteristics
   B. barriers to participation
   C. existing resources
   D. profiles of competing resources

2. Research has demonstrated that of the following, the MOST effective medium for communicating with external publics is(are)
   A. video news releases
   B. television
   C. radio
   D. newspapers

3. Basic ideas behind the effort to influence the attitudes and behaviors of a constituency include each of the following EXCEPT the idea that
   A. words, rather than actions or events, are most likely to motivate
   B. demands for action are a usual response
   C. self-interest usually figures heavily into public involvement
   D. the reliability of change programs is difficult to assess

4. An agency representative is trying to craft a pithy message to constituents in order to encourage the use of agency program resources.
   Choosing an audience for such messages is easiest when the message
   A. is project- or behavior-based
   B. is combined with other messages
   C. is abstract
   D. has a broad appeal

5. Of the following factors, the MOST important to the success of an agency's external education or communication programs is the
   A. amount of resources used to implement them
   B. public's prior experiences with the agency
   C. real value of the program to the public
   D. commitment of the internal audience

6. A representative for a state agency is being interviewed by a reporter from a local news network. The representative is being asked to defend a program that is extremely unpopular in certain parts of the municipality.
   When a constituency is known to be opposed to a position, the MOST useful communication strategy is to present

A. only the arguments that are consistent with constituents' views
B. only the agency's side of the issue
C. both sides of the argument as clearly as possible
D. both sides of the argument, omitting key information about the opposing position

7. The MOST significant barriers to effective agency community relations include
   I. widespread distrust of communication strategies
   II. the media's "watchdog" stance
   III. public apathy
   IV. statutory opposition

   The CORRECT answer is:
   A. I only   B. I and II   C. II and III   D. III and IV

7._____

8. In conducting an education program, many agencies use workshops and seminars in a classroom setting.
   Advantages of classroom-style teaching over other means of educating the public include each of the following, EXCEPT
   A. enabling an instructor to verify learning through testing and interaction with the target audience
   B. enabling hands-on practice and other participatory learning techniques
   C. ability to reach an unlimited number of participants in a given length of time
   D. ability to convey the latest, most up-to-date information

8._____

9. The _____ model of community relations is characterized by an attempt to persuade the public to adopt the agency's point of view.
   A. two-way symmetric   B. two-way asymmetric
   C. public information   D. press agency/publicity

9._____

10. Important elements of an internal situation analysis include the
    I. list of agency opponents   II. communication audit
    III. updated organizational almanac   IV. stakeholder analysis

    The CORRECT answer is:
    A. I and II   B. I, II, and III   C. II and III   D. I, II, III and IV

10._____

11. Government agency information efforts typically involve each of the following objectives, EXCEPT to
    A. implement changes in the policies of government agencies to align with public opinion
    B. communicate the work of agencies
    C. explain agency techniques in a way that invites input from citizens
    D. provide citizen feedback to government administrators

11._____

12. Factors that are likely to influence the effectiveness of an educational campaign include the
    I. level of homogeneity among intended participants
    II. number and types of media used
    III. receptivity of the intended participants
    IV. level of specificity in the message or behavior to be taught

    The CORRECT answer is:
    A. I and II   B. I, II, and III   C. II and III   D. I, II, III, and IV

13. An agency representative is writing instructional objectives that will later help to measure the effectiveness of an educational program.
    Which of the following verbs, included in an objective, would be MOST helpful for the purpose of measuring effectiveness?
    A. Know   B. Identify   C. Learn   D. Comprehend

14. A state education agency wants to encourage participation in a program that has just received a boost through new federal legislation. The program is intended to include participants from a wide variety of socioeconomic and other demographic characteristics. The agency wants to launch a broad-based program that will inform virtually every interested party in the state about the program's new circumstances.
    In attempting to deliver this message to such a wide-ranging constituency, the agency's BEST practice would be to
    A. broadcast the same message through as many different media channels as possible
    B. focus on one discrete segment of the public at a time
    C. craft a message whose appeal is as broad as the public itself
    D. let the program's achievements speak for themselves and rely on word-of-mouth

15. Advantages associated with using the World Wide Web as an educational tool include
    I. an appeal to younger generations of the public
    II. visually-oriented, interactive learning
    III. learning that is not confined by space, time, or institutional association
    IV. a variety of methods for verifying use and learning

    The CORRECT answer is:
    A. I only   B. I and II   C. I, II, and III   D. I, II, II, and IV

16. In agencies involved in health care, community relations is a critical function because it
    A. serves as an intermediary between the agency and consumers
    B. generates a clear mission statement for agency goals and priorities
    C. ensures patient privacy while satisfying the media's right to information
    D. helps marketing professionals determine the wants and needs of agency constituents

17. After an extensive campaign to promote its newest program to constituents, an agency learns that most of the audience did not understand the intended message.
MOST likely, the agency has
   A. chosen words that were intended to inform, rather than persuade
   B. not accurately interpreted what the audience really needed to know
   C. overestimated the ability of the audience to receive and process the message
   D. compensated for noise that may have interrupted the message

18. The necessary elements that lead to conviction and motivation in the minds of participants in an educational or information program include each of the following, EXCEPT the _____ of the message.
   A. acceptability
   B. intensity
   C. single-channel appeal
   D. pervasiveness

19. Printed materials are often at the core of educational programs provided by public agencies.
The PRIMARY disadvantage associated with print is that it
   A. does not enable comprehensive treatment of a topic
   B. is generally unreliable in term of assessing results
   C. is often the most expensive medium available
   D. is constrained by time

20. Traditional thinking on public opinion holds that there is about _____ percent of the public who are pivotal to shifting the balance and momentum of opinion—they are concerned about an issue, but not fanatical, and interested enough to pay attention to a reasoned discussion.
   A. 2   B. 10   C. 33   D. 51

21. One of the most useful guidelines for influencing attitude change among people is to
   A. invite the target audience to come to you, rather than approaching them
   B. use moral appeals as the primary approach
   C. use concrete images to enable people to see the results of behaviors or indifference
   D. offer tangible rewards to people for changes in behavior

22. An agency is attempting to evaluate the effectiveness of its educational program. For this purpose, it wants to observe several focus groups discussing the same program.
Which of the following would NOT be a guideline for the use of focus groups?
   A. Focus groups should only include those who have participated in the program.
   B. Be sure to accurately record the discussion.
   C. The same questions should be asked at each focus group meeting.
   D. It is often helpful to have a neutral, non-agency employee facilitate discussions.

23. Research consistently shows that _____ is the determinant most likely to make a newspaper editor run a news release.
    A. novelty   B. prominence   C. proximity   D. conflict

24. Which of the following is NOT one of the major variables to take into account when considering a population-needs assessment?
    A. State of program development   B. Resources available
    C. Demographics   D. Community attitudes

25. The FIRST step in any communications audit is to
    A. develop a research instrument
    B. determine how the organization currently communicates
    C. hire a contractor
    D. determine which audience to assess

KEY (CORRECT ANSWERS)

1.	A		11.	A
2.	D		12.	D
3.	A		13.	B
4.	A		14.	B
5.	D		15.	C
6.	C		16.	A
7.	D		17.	B
8.	C		18.	C
9.	B		19.	B
10.	C		20.	B

21. C
22. A
23. C
24. C
25. D

TEST 2

DIRECTIONS: Each question or incomplete statement is followed by several suggested answers or completions. Select the one that BEST answers the question or completes the statement. *PRINT THE LETTER OF THE CORRECT ANSWER IN THE SPACE AT THE RIGHT.*

1. A public relations practitioner at an agency has just composed a press release highlighting a program's recent accomplishments and success stories.
   In pitching such releases to print outlets, the practitioner should
   I. e-mail, mail, or send them by messenger
   II. address them to "editor" or "news director"
   III. have an assistant call all media contacts by telephone
   IV. ask reporters or editors how they prefer to receive them

   The CORRECT answer is:
   A. I and II   B. I and IV   C. II, III, and IV   D. III only

2. The "output goals" of an educational program are MOST likely to include
   A. specified ratings of services by participants on a standardized scale
   B. observable effects on a given community or clientele
   C. the number of instructional hours provided
   D. the number of participants served

3. An agency wants to evaluate satisfaction levels among program participants, and mails out questionnaires to everyone who has been enrolled in the last year.
   The PRIMARY problem associated with this method of evaluative research is that it
   A. poses a significant inconvenience for respondents
   B. is inordinately expensive
   C. does not allow for follow-up or clarification questions
   D. usually involves a low response rate

4. A communications audit is an important tool for measuring
   A. the depth of penetration of a particular message or program
   B. the cost of the organization's information campaigns
   C. how key audiences perceive an organization
   D. the commitment of internal stakeholders

5. The "ABCs" of written learning objectives include each of the following, EXCEPT
   A. Audience   B. Behavior   C. Conditions   D. Delineation

6. When attempting to change the behaviors of constituents, it is important to keep in mind that
   I. most people are skeptical of communications that try to get them to change their behaviors
   II. in most cases, a person selects the media to which he exposes himself
   III. people tend to react defensively to messages or programs that rely on fear as a motivating factor
   IV. programs should aim for the broadest appeal possible in order to include as many participants as possible

   The CORRECT answer is:
   A. I and II   B. I, II and III   C. II and III   D. I, II, III, and IV

7. The "laws" of public opinion include the idea that it is
   A. useful for anticipating emergencies
   B. not sensitive to important events
   C. basically determined by self-interest
   D. sustainable through persistent appeals

8. Which of the following types of evaluations is used to measure public attitudes before and after an information/educational program?
   A. Retrieval study
   B. Copy test
   C. Quota sampling
   D. Benchmark study

9. The PRIMARY source for internal communications is(are) usually
   A. flow charts
   B. meetings
   C. voice mail
   D. printed publications

10. An agency representative is putting together informational materials—brochures and a newsletter—outlining changes in one of the state's biggest benefits programs.
    In assembling print materials as a medium for delivering information to the public, the representative should keep in mind each of the following trends:
    I. For various reasons, the reading capabilities of the public are in general decline
    II. Without tables and graphs to help illustrate the changes, it is unlikely that the message will be delivered effectively
    III. Professionals and career-oriented people are highly receptive to information written in the form of a journal article or empirical study
    IV. People tend to be put off by print materials that use itemized and bulleted (●) lists

    The CORRECT answer is:
    A. I and II   B. I, II and III   C. II and III   D. I, II, III, and IV

11. Which of the following steps in a problem-oriented information campaign would typically be implemented FIRST?
    A. Deciding on tactics
    B. Determining a communications strategy
    C. Evaluating the problem's impact
    D. Developing an organizational strategy

12. A common pitfall in conducting an educational program is to
    A. aim it at the wrong target audience
    B. overfund it
    C. leave it in the hands of people who are in the business of education, rather than those with expertise in the business of the organization
    D. ignore the possibility that some other organization is meeting the same educational need for the target audience

13. The key factors that affect the credibility of an agency's educational program include
    A. organization
    B. scope
    C. sophistication
    D. penetration

14. Research on public opinion consistently demonstrates that it is
    A. easy to move people toward a strong opinion on anything, as long as they are approached directly through their emotions
    B. easier to move people away from an opinion they currently hold than to have them form an opinion about something they have not previously cared about
    C. easy to move people toward a strong opinion on anything, as long as the message appeals to their reason and intellect
    D. difficult to move people toward a strong opinion on anything, no matter what the approach

15. In conducting an education program, many agencies use meetings and conferences to educate an audience about the organization and its programs. Advantages associated with this approach include
    I. a captive audience that is known to be interested in the topic
    II. ample opportunities for verifying learning
    III. cost-efficient meeting space
    IV. the ability to provide information on a wider variety of subjects

    The CORRECT answer is:
    A. I and II   B. I, III and IV   C. II and III   D. I, II, III and IV

16. An agency is attempting to evaluate the effectiveness of its educational programs. For this purpose, it wants to observe several focus groups discussing particular programs.
    For this purpose, a focus group should never number more than _____ participants.
    A. 5   B. 10   C. 15   D. 20

17. A _____ speech is written so that several agency members can deliver it to different audiences with only minor variations.
    A. basic B. printed C. quota D. pattern

18. Which of the following statements about public opinion is generally considered to be FALSE?
    A. Opinion is primarily reactive rather than proactive.
    B. People have more opinions about goals than about the means by which to achieve them.
    C. Facts tend to shift opinion in the accepted direction when opinion is not solidly structured.
    D. Public opinion is based more on information than desire.

19. An agency is trying to promote its educational program.
    As a general rule, the agency should NOT assume that
    A. people will only participate if they perceive an individual benefit
    B. promotions need to be aimed at small, discrete groups
    C. if the program is good, the audience will find out about it
    D. a variety of methods, including advertising, special events, and direct mail, should be considered

20. In planning a successful educational program, probably the first and most important question for an agency to ask is:
    A. What will be the content of the program?
    B. Who will be served by the program?
    C. When is the best time to schedule the program?
    D. Why is the program necessary?

21. Media kits are LEAST likely to contain
    A. fact sheets   B. memoranda
    C. photographs with captions D. news releases

22. The use of pamphlets and booklets as media for communication with the public often involves the disadvantage that
    A. the messages contained within them are frequently nonspecific
    B. it is difficult to measure their effectiveness in delivering the message
    C. there are few opportunities for people to refer to them
    D. color reproduction is poor

23. The MOST important prerequisite of a good educational program is an
    A. abundance of resources to implement it
    B. individual staff unit formed for the purpose of program delivery
    C. accurate needs assessment
    D. uneducated constituency

24. After an education program has been delivered, an agency conducts a program evaluation to determine whether its objectives have been met.
General rules about how to conduct such an education program valuation include each of the following, EXCEPT that it
    A. must be done immediately after the program has been implemented
    B. should be simple and easy to use
    C. should be designed so that tabulation of responses can take place quickly and inexpensively
    D. should solicit mostly subjective, open-ended responses if the audience was large

25. Using electronic media such as television as means of educating the public is typically recommended ONLY for agencies that
    I. have a fairly simple message to begin with
    II. want to reach the masses, rather than a targeted audience
    III. have substantial financial resources
    IV. accept that they will not be able to measure the results of the campaign with much precision

    The CORRECT answer is:
    A. I and II   B. I, II and III   C. II and IV   D. I, II, III and IV

KEY (CORRECT ANSWERS)

1.	B	11.	C
2.	C	12.	D
3.	D	13.	A
4.	C	14.	D
5.	D	15.	B
6.	B	16.	B
7.	C	17.	D
8.	D	18.	D
9.	D	19.	C
10.	A	20.	D

21.	B
22.	B
23.	C
24.	D
25.	D

READING COMPREHENSION
UNDERSTANDING AND INTERPRETING WRITTEN MATERIAL
EXAMINATION SECTION
TEST 1

DIRECTIONS: Each question or incomplete statement is followed by several suggested answers or completions. Select the one that BEST answers the question or completes the statement. *PRINT THE LETTER OF THE CORRECT ANSWER IN THE SPACE AT THE RIGHT.*

Questions 1-4.

DIRECTIONS: Questions 1 through 4 are to be answered ONLY according to the information given in the following passage.

HANDLING HOSPITAL LAUNDRY

In a hospital, care must be taken when handling laundry in order to reduce the chance of germs spreading. There is always the possibility that dirty laundry will be carrying dangerous germs. To avoid catching germs when they are working with dirty laundry, laundry workers should be sure that any cuts or wounds they have are bandaged before they touch the dirty laundry. They should also be careful when handling this laundry not to rub their eyes, nose, or mouth. Just like all other hospital workers, laundry workers should also protect themselves against germs by washing and rinsing their hands thoroughly before eating meals and before leaving work at the end of the day.

To be sure that germs from dirty laundry do not pass onto clean laundry and thereby increase the danger to patients, clean and dirty laundry should not be handled near each other or by the same person. Special care also has to be taken with laundry that comes from a patient who has a dangerous, highly contagious disease so that as few people as possible come in direct contact with this laundry. Laundry from this patient, therefore, should be kept separate from other dirty laundry at all times.

1. According to the above passage, when working with dirty laundry, laundry workers should

    A. destroy laundry carrying dangerous germs
    B. have any cuts bandaged before touching the dirty laundry
    C. never touch the dirty laundry directly
    D. rub their eyes, nose, and mouth to protect them from germs

2. According to the above passage, all hospital workers should wash their hands thoroughly

    A. after eating meals to remove any trace of food from their hands
    B. at every opportunity to show good example to the patients
    C. before eating meals to protect themselves against germs
    D. before starting work in the morning to feel fresh and ready to do a good day's work

3. According to the above passage, the danger to patients will increase

   A. unless a worker handles dirty and clean laundry at the same time
   B. unless clean and dirty laundry are handled near each other
   C. when clean laundry is ironed frequently
   D. when germs pass from dirty laundry to clean laundry

4. According to the above passage, laundry from a patient with a dangerous, highly contagious disease should be

   A. given special care so that as few people as possible come in direct contact with it
   B. handled in the same way as any other dirty laundry
   C. washed by hand
   D. separated from the other dirty laundry just before it is washed

Questions 5-8.

DIRECTIONS: Questions 5 through 8 are to be answered ONLY according to the information given in the following passage.

MARKING PROCEDURES FOR PERSONAL WASH

As soon as a bundle of personal wash is brought into the laundry, it is taken to a marking section. Here an employee marks the individual pieces so that pieces following different courses through the laundry may be brought together when work upon them has been completed. The wash is identified either by visible markings, invisible markings, or by labels. Serial numbers and letters, often coded identifying the wash, are marked upon each article.

Visible markings should be placed on the concealed parts of the wash, such as trouser waistbands, either with a marking pencil or by a machine with a keyboard which looks like a typewriter. A similar machine is also used in laundries to mark pieces with invisible ink. These marks need not be concealed since they can be seen only under ultraviolet light. Labels with the markings on them, may be stapled or sewed onto each piece of wash. In addition to identifying, the marker has the task of listing, counting, and marking on a printed laundry list each piece in the bundle. After the wash has been marked, the marker then classifies the wash into groups that can be laundered together.

This is the only work done in the marking section.

5. According to the above passage, an IMPORTANT reason for placing identifying marks on personal wash is to

   A. keep a correct record of how many pounds of laundry are washed
   B. make sure that all the pieces in the bundle of laundry are washed together
   C. classify the pieces in the bundle according to the way they are washed
   D. make it possible to bring together later pieces that are washed separately

6. According to the above passage, in order to see a laundry mark made with invisible ink, it is necessary to

   A. use an ultraviolet light   B. wet it
   C. use a special machine   D. treat it with a mild acid

7. According to the above passage, an advantage of using invisible ink to mark laundry is that

   A. it is cheaper
   B. the mark can be made with an ordinary pencil
   C. the mark can be put any place on the wash and doesn't have to be hidden
   D. it takes less time to do the marking

8. According to the above passage, the marker does NOT

   A. put identifying marks on the wash
   B. sew small rips in torn wash
   C. check the number of pieces in each bundle of wash
   D. group the pieces of wash that can be laundered together

Questions 9-12.

DIRECTIONS: Questions 9 through 12 are to be answered ONLY according to the information given in the following passage.

THE HANDLING OF RAYON IN THE LAUNDRY

Rayon is an artificial fabric manufactured from wood pulp and short cotton fibres. It is extensively used in such items as shirtings, dress goods, and curtains, and may compose the entire fabric or simply be a part of the weave. While quite strong and substantial in its dry state, rayon is weak when wet and must, therefore, be handled with great care in the washing process. It should not be rubbed or stretched and should always be placed in nets to relieve as much strain as possible while in the washwheel. Rayon should preferably be washed in cold water with the proper materials for cold water washing. If there is any doubt as to whether a fabric is silk or rayon, a small thread or particle may be burnt. If it is silk, the threads will burn slowly and leave a small ball of ash at the end of the thread. Rayon, however, burns quickly and leaves no ash or telltale ball.

9. According to the above passage, rayon is made from a combination of _____ and _____

   A. wood; silk   B. wool; linen
   C. cotton; wood   D. silk; linen

10. According to the above passage, a manufacturer would probably NOT use rayon to make

    A. kitchen window curtains   B. dish towels
    C. nurses' uniforms   D. men's shirts

11. According to the above passage, the MAIN reason for putting rayon fabrics in a net when they are to be washed is that rayon is

    A. washable only in cold water
    B. a manufactured fabric
    C. easily stained by the materials from the washwheel
    D. not a strong material when wet

12. According to the above passage, threads of rayon burn _____ and leave _____ ash.

   A. slowly; no
   B. fast; no
   C. slowly; a ball of
   D. fast; a ball of

Questions 13-17.

DIRECTIONS: Questions 13 through 17 are to be answered ONLY according to the information given in the following paragraph.

REPORT FOR THE YEAR 2005 - LAUNDRY DIVISION

The Area A Central Laundry, which cost about 4½ million dollars with the equipment, was opened in December 2005, enabling the Department of Hospitals to close a number of out-of-date laundries in some Area A hospitals. The new Area A Central Laundry can now process 8,000 pounds of linen in an hour, or about 17½ million pounds a year. It has sufficient space for additional equipment to increase the capacity to 10,000 pounds per hour. The cost of processing laundry in 2004 at the old laundries was about twelve cents per pound. However, in 2005, the cost at the new laundry was about six cents per pound. Area A now does all the laundry for the municipal hospitals in that city and for the Area B Hospital Center.

During 2005, the laundries in Area C, D, E, and F Hospitals were also shut down and their work assigned to Area G laundry. About one-quarter of the original laundry staff was retained at each hospital to sort soiled linen and distribute clean linen — the other employees were reassigned to other laundries.

13. According to the above passage, can the new Area A Central Laundry do more than 8,000 pounds of linen an hour?

   A. Yes, if it gets more equipment
   B. Yes, only if it gets more space
   C. No, 8,000 pounds is the maximum capacity
   D. It is not possible to find this out from the passage

14. According to the above passage, the cost of processing laundry at the new Area A Laundry in 2005, as compared with the cost at the old laundries in 2004, was

   A. twice as much
   B. about the same
   C. about half
   D. only slightly less

15. According to the above passage, the cost of processing laundry in the new laundry was

   A. greater than at the old laundries
   B. equal to the cost at the laundries in Area C, D, E, and F Hospitals
   C. greater by 10,000 pounds per hour
   D. less by more than five cents per pound

16. According to the above passage, dirty linen from Area E Hospital is now laundred at the Area

   A. G laundry
   B. A Central Laundry
   C. B Center Laundry
   D. E Hospital

17. According to the above passage, what happened to the laundry workers at Area F Hospital when the laundry there was shut down? 17.____

    A. One-quarter of them went to Area A Central Laundry and the rest to the Area G laundry.
    B. Half of them were given jobs in other municipal departments and the rest were sent to other laundries.
    C. About three-quarters of them went to work at other laundries in the department.
    D. All of them were assigned to other hospital laundries to work on sorting and giving out laundry.

Questions 18-22.

DIRECTIONS: Questions 18 through 22 are to be answered ONLY according to the information given in the following paragraph.

The fact that your hospital has been ordered to make certain budgetary cutbacks has angered and frightened the community. A peaceful demonstration has been taking place for the last three days on hospital grounds. The group's leader has met with the hospital administrator; and although the meeting was amicable, nothing was resolved and the community still feels abused by the hospital, the health and hospitals corporation, and the city. Because you fear that the demonstration may become violent, you arrange to discuss first with the hospital administration and then with your staff what actions may become necessary.

18. Which of the following actions SHOULD be included in your preliminary plans? 18.____

    A. Notifying the media of a possible altercation at the hospital.
    B. Determining the location of the command post.
    C. Blocking all entrances and exits to the facility with furniture.
    D. Calling the administration and ordering them to leave the premises immediately.

19. Of the following, which is the MOST important topic you should discuss with your subordinates prior to the possible increased activity by the community? 19.____

    A. The nature of the group's complaints against the hospital and the city
    B. Your view on the hospital's position in this matter
    C. The need for self-control by all security personnel
    D. Hand-to-hand fighting techniques which may be necessary if the community group becomes violent

20. Assume that your concerns prove correct and the demonstration becomes less organized, less controlled, and potentially violent. 20.____
    As the supervisor of security personnel, your CHIEF responsibility is to

    A. join your men in quelling any disturbance
    B. maintain a clearly defined chain of command so that orders remain clear and concise
    C. prevent the demonstration's leaders from entering the hospital administration building so that hospital routines may continue without interruption
    D. meet with demonstration leaders as soon as possible

21. The one of the following choices that contains only the MOST important items of information a security officer should transmit to his hospital administrator in the situation described above is the   21.___

    A. approximate size of the group of demonstrators, the security measures already taken, and the number of officers on duty
    B. number of available parking spaces, the demands of the demonstrators, and the names of community leaders seen
    C. number of officers on leave, the number of patients in the hospital, and the approximate size of the group of demonstrators
    D. number of officers on leave, the demands of the demonstrators, and the number of plant maintenance staff on duty

22. Of the following, the area whose security is LEAST important to protect during the demonstrations is the   22.___

    A. pharmacy
    B. patients' accounts office
    C. pathology laboratory
    D. linen storage rooms

Questions 23-25.

DIRECTIONS: Questions 23 through 25 are to be answered ONLY according to the information given in the following statement.

When a voluntary hospital admits a Blue Cross subscriber who has been referred from a city hospital, a concurrent submission of the case shall be made by it to both Blue Cross and the city Investigator who routinely visits the voluntary hospital. This procedure will be advantageous to both the voluntary hospital and the city since the hospital would be notified immediately of the ability of the city to reimburse should Blue Cross coverage be inapplicable or insufficient. Furthermore, the city will be able to assure itself of potential State Aid for those cases for whom it may have to assume some responsibility. Necessary time limits to process applications for State Aid can also be made if this referral is concurrent, such as for state charges and relief clients, who are frequently Blue Cross members. This investigation can best be conducted by the city staff assigned to the voluntary hospital, rather than by the staff in the referring Municipal hospital.

23. According to the above statement, one responsibility of a voluntary hospital with respect to an admission who is a Blue Cross subscriber is to   23.___

    A. get the city to reimburse its fair share if Blue Cross coverage is inapplicable or insufficient
    B. refer the case to the city hospital for possible collection of State Aid
    C. submit the case concurrently to both Blue Cross and the city Investigator
    D. submit the case to the city investigator if the patient has been referred by a city hospital

24. According to the above statement, it is NOT an advantage of the procedure described that the   24.___

    A. city can make sure of getting possible State Aid for those cases for whom it may be partly responsible
    B. cost of caring for the cases referred to will be shared by Blue Cross, the Voluntary hospital, the city, and the State
    C. needed time limits to handle State Aid applications can be made
    D. Voluntary hospitals will know immediately if the city will pay for its referrals who do not have enough Blue Cross coverage

25. According to the above statement, the investigation referred to can be carried out MOST advantageously by the

   A. city investigator who routinely visits the Voluntary hospital
   B. city staff assigned to the hospital that admitted the patient
   C. staff of the hospital that referred the patient
   D. staff of the Voluntary hospital that accepted the referral

KEY (CORRECT ANSWERS)

1. B		11. D
2. C		12. B
3. D		13. A
4. A		14. C
5. D		15. D
6. A		16. A
7. C		17. C
8. B		18. B
9. C		19. C
10. B		20. B

21. A
22. D
23. D
24. B
25. B

TEST 2

DIRECTIONS: Each question consists of a statement. You are to indicate whether the statement is TRUE (T) or FALSE (F). *PRINT THE LETTER OF THE CORRECT ANSWER IN THE SPACE AT THE RIGHT.*

Questions 1-9.

DIRECTIONS: Questions 1 through 9 are to be answered SOLELY on the basis of the information contained in the following passage.

All deaths must be reported to the Department of Health by the licensed physician in attendance at the time of death if death is from natural causes and does not occur in a hospital, or by the person in charge of a hospital if the death occurs there from natural causes, or by the office of the chief medical examiner if the death is apparently from other than natural causes such as violence or suicide. The physician in attendance or the person in charge of a hospital must file a death certificate accompanied by a confidential medical report. The office of the medical examiner files only a death certificate. These papers should be filed within twenty-four hours after death or finding of the remains, with the office of the Department of Health in the borough in which the death occurs or in which the remains are found. However, this requirement is also considered fulfilled if such papers are delivered immediately upon demand and within the twenty-four hours either to a funeral director or undertaker authorized to take charge of the remains or to the city superintendent of mortuaries for those cases in which the remains are to be buried in the city cemetery. These persons receiving the papers must then file the certificates and confidential report with the Department of Health within 48 hours following death or the finding of the remains.

1. A death from heart disease at home must be reported to the Department of Health by the licensed physician in attendance at the time of death.   1.___

2. All deaths outside a hospital must be reported to the Department of Health by the physician in attendance.   2.___

3. The Police Department reports all violent deaths to the Department of Health.   3.___

4. When the death is a suicide, a confidential medical report is filed by the medical examiner.   4.___

5. If a person dies in a hospital from other than natural causes, the death certificate must be filed by the office of the medical examiner.   5.___

6. If a person who lives in Brooklyn dies in Manhattan, the death certificate must be filed in Manhattan.   6.___

7. The physician in attendance who is required to file a death certificate must do so within 24 hours after the death.   7.___

8. The death certificate may also be delivered to an authorized undertaker instead of filing it directly with the Department of Health.   8.___

9. The authorized funeral director who has the death certificate must file it with the Department of Health within twenty-four hours after he has received it.   9.___

Questions 10-22.

DIRECTIONS: Questions 10 through 22 are to be answered SOLELY on the basis of the information contained in the following paragraph.

THE HUMAN BODY

The vertebrae of the spinal column all have the same general shape in that each has a thick body of bone in front, from the sides of which two lighter extensions of bone pass backwards and around to join each other, thus forming an opening in the center. These openings, placed in line with each other as in an intact spinal column, help form the spinal canal which encloses and protects the spinal cord. Cartilage plates between the bodies of the upper twenty-four vertebrae permit considerable movement of the vertebrae and cushion the shock of falling. The sternum is a long, flat bone forming the middle part of the chest's front wall. The upper end of the sternum is a long, flat bone forming the middle part of the chest's front wall. The upper end of the sternum supports the collarbones, and most of the ribs on each side of the chest are attached to the sternum by means of cartilage. Each of the twelve ribs on each side of the chest's bony framework is joined to the spinal column by a movable joint. The first seven ribs, on each side, called true ribs, are joined in front to the sternum by cartilage, and the next three, called false ribs, are each joined similarly to the rib immediately above. The lowest two, called floating ribs, are not fastened at all by their front ends. The pelvis, a basin-shaped ring of bones, is located between the movable vertebrae of the spinal column, which it supports, and the lower limbs, on which it rests. The pelvis, forming the floor of the abdominal cavity and providing deep pockets into which the heads of the thighbones fit, consists of four bones: the sacrum and coccyx behind, and the two hip bones at the sides and front.

10. The vertebrae have a bony part only in the front.   10.____

11. The spinal cord passes through the openings in the center of the vertebrae.   11.____

12. The total number of ribs in the body is 24.   12.____

13. The spinal cord is made up of the openings in the vertebrae.   13.____

14. The shock of falling is eased by cartilage plates between the vertebrae.   14.____

15. The sternum is at the rear of the chest cavity.   15.____

16. The collarbones are supported by the top part of the sternum.   16.____

17. All the ribs are joined in the front to the sternum by cartilage.   17.____

18. The floating ribs are not fastened to the spinal column at all.   18.____

19. The pelvis is a bony structure.   19.____

20. The hip bones are a part of the pelvis.   20.____

21. The pelvis is at the bottom of the abdominal cavity.   21.____

Questions 22-26.

DIRECTIONS: Questions 22 through 26 are to be answered SOLELY on the basis of the information contained in the following paragraph.

RELEASE OF HUMAN REMAINS FROM CITY MORTUARY

When human remains which have been removed to the city mortuary are subsequently claimed, the superintendent of city mortuaries shall deliver the remains, on demand, only to a funeral director or undertaker. The latter must submit a written statement that he or the funeral establishment with which he is associated has been employed by the next of kin, legal representative, or, in the absence of arrangements by such next of kin or legal representative, by a friend of the deceased. Together with the remains, the superintendent shall deliver the certificate of death or fetal death and confidential medical report, if any, or, any permit issued by the Department authorizing burial in the city cemetery. No burial permit may be issued unless the certificate of death has been filed with the Department of Health.

22. To secure the release of human remains from the city mortuary, the next of kin must advise the mortuaries superintendent by telephone of the name of the undertaker. 22.___

23. The superintendent of city mortuaries cannot release a body directly to the next of kin. 23.___

24. If there is a confidential medical report, the superintendent of city mortuaries is supposed to deliver this with the body to the person authorized to receive the body. 24.___

25. The permit for burial in the city cemetery is shown to the duly employed undertaker, but is kept by the superintendent of city mortuaries. 25.___

26. If a certificate of death has not been filed with the Department of Health, no burial permit may be issued. 26.___

Questions 27-30.

DIRECTIONS: Questions 27 through 30 are to be answered SOLELY on the basis of the information given in this paragraph.

CARBON MONOXIDE GAS

Carbon monoxide is a deadly gas from the effects of which no one is immune. Any person's strength will be cut down considerably by breathing this gas, even though he does not take in enough to overcome him. Wearing a handkerchief tied around the nose and mouth offers some protection against the irritating fumes of ordinary smoke, but many people have died convinced that a handkerchief will stop carbon monoxide. Any person entering a room filled with this deadly gas should wear a mask equipped with an air hose, or even better, an oxygen breathing apparatus.

27. Some people get no ill effects from carbon monoxide gas until they are overcome. 27.___

28. A person can die from breathing carbon monoxide gas. 28.___

29. A handkerchief around the mouth and nose gives some protection against the effects of ordinary smoke. 29._____

30. It is better for a person entering a room filled with carbon monoxide to wear a mask equipped with an air hose than an oxygen breathing apparatus. 30._____

KEY (CORRECT ANSWERS)

1.	T	16.	T
2.	F	17.	F
3.	F	18.	F
4.	F	19.	T
5.	T	20.	T
6.	T	21.	T
7.	T	22.	F
8.	T	23.	T
9.	F	24.	T
10.	F	25.	F
11.	T	26.	T
12.	T	27.	F
13.	T	28.	T
14.	T	29.	T
15.	F	30.	F

PREPARING WRITTEN MATERIAL

PARAGRAPH REARRANGEMENT
COMMENTARY

The sentences that follow are in scrambled order. You are to rearrange them in proper order and indicate the letter choice containing the correct answer at the space at the right.

Each group of sentences in this section is actually a paragraph presented in scrambled order. Each sentence in the group has a place in that paragraph; no sentence is to be left out. You are to read each group of sentences and decide upon the best order in which to put the sentences so as to form a well-organized paragraph.

The questions in this section measure the ability to solve a problem when all the facts relevant to its solution are not given.

More specifically, certain positions of responsibility and authority require the employee to discover connection between events sometimes, apparently, unrelated. In order to do this, the employee will find it necessary to correctly infer that unspecified events have probably occurred or are likely to occur. This ability becomes especially important when action must be taken on incomplete information.

Accordingly, these questions require competitors to choose among several suggested alternatives, each of which presents a different sequential arrangement of the events. Competitors must choose the MOST logical of the suggested sequences.

In order to do so, they may be required to draw on general knowledge to infer missing concepts or events that are essential to sequencing the given events. Competitors should be careful to infer only what is essential to the sequence. The plausibility of the wrong alternatives will always require the inclusion of unlikely events or of additional chains of events which are NOT essential to sequencing the given events.

It's very important to remember that you are looking for the best of the four possible choices, and that the best choice of all may not even be one of the answers you're given to choose from.

There is no one right way to solve these problems. Many people have found it helpful to first write out the order of the sentences, as they would have arranged them, on their scrap paper before looking at the possible answers. If their optimum answer is there, this can save them some time. If it isn't, this method can still give insight into solving the problem. Others find it most helpful to just go through each of the possible choices, contrasting each as they go along. You should use whatever method feels comfortable and works for you.

While most of these types of questions are not that difficult, we've added a higher percentage of the difficult type, just to give you more practice. Usually there are only one or two questions on this section that contain such subtle distinctions that you're unable to answer confidently. And you then may find yourself stuck deciding between two possible choices, neither of which you're sure about.

EXAMINATION SECTION
TEST 1

DIRECTIONS: The following groups of sentences need to be arranged in an order that makes sense. Select the letter preceding the sequence that represents the BEST sentence order. *PRINT THE LETTER OF THE CORRECT ANSWER IN THE SPACE AT THE RIGHT.*

1. I. The keyboard was purposely designed to be a little awkward to slow typists down.
    II. The arrangement of letters on the keyboard of a typewriter was not designed for the convenience of the typist.
    III. Fortunately, no one is suggesting that a new keyboard be designed right away.
    IV. If one were, we would have to learn to type all over again.
    V. The reason was that the early machines were slower than the typists and would jam easily.
    The CORRECT answer is:
    A. I, III, IV, II, V
    B. II, V, I, IV, III
    C. V, I, II, III, IV
    D. II, I, V, III, IV

2. I. The majority of the new service jobs are part-time or low-paying.
    II. According to the U.S. Bureau of Labor Statistics, jobs in the service sector constitute 72% of all jobs in this country.
    III. If more and more workers receive less and less money, who will buy the goods and services needed to keep the economy going?
    IV. The service sector is by far the fastest growing part of the United States economy.
    V. Some economists look upon this trend with great concern.
    The CORRECT answer is:
    A. II, IV, I, V, III
    B. II, III, IV, I, V
    C. V, IV, II, III, I
    D. III, I, II, IV, V

3. I. They can also affect one's endurance.
    II. This can stabilize blood sugar levels, and ensure that the brain is receiving a steady, constant, supply of glucose, so that one is *hitting on all cylinders* while taking the test.
    III. By food, we mean real food, not junk food or unhealthy snacks.
    IV. For this reason, it is important not to skip a meal, and to bring food with you to the exam.
    V. One's blood sugar levels can affect how clearly one is able to think and concentrate during an exam.
    The CORRECT answer is:
    A. V, IV, II, III, I
    B. V, II, I, IV, III
    C. V, I, IV, III, II
    D. V, IV, I, III, II

4.
I. Those who are the embodiment of desire are absorbed in material quests, and those who are the embodiment of feeling are warriors who value power more than possession.
II. These qualities are in everyone, but in different degrees.
III. But those who value understanding yearn not for goods or victory, but for knowledge.
IV. According to Plato, human behavior flows from three main sources: desire, emotion, and knowledge.
V. In the perfect state, the industrial forces would produce but not rule, the military would protect but not rule, and the forces of knowledge, the philosopher kings, would reign.
The CORRECT answer is:
A. IV, V, I, II, III
B. V, I, II, III, IV
C. IV, III, II, I, V
D. IV, II, I, III, V

4.____

5.
I. Of the more than 26,000 tons of garbage produced daily in New York City, 12,000 tons arrive daily at Fresh Kills.
II. In a month, enough garbage accumulates there to fill the Empire State Building.
III. In 1937, the Supreme Court halted the practice of dumping the trash of New York City into the sea.
IV. Although the garbage is compacted, in a few years the mounds of garbage at Fresh Kills will be the highest points south of Maine's Mount Desert Island on the Eastern Seaboard.
V. Instead, tugboats now pull barges of much of the trash to Staten Island and the largest landfill in the world, Fresh Kills.
The CORRECT answer is:
A. III, V, IV, I, II
B. III, V, II, IV, I
C. III, V, I, II, IV
D. III, II, V, IV, I

5.____

6.
I. Communists rank equality very high, but freedom very low.
II. Unlike communists, conservatives place a high value on freedom and a very low value on equality.
III. A recent study demonstrated that one way to classify people's political beliefs is to look at the importance placed on two words: freedom and equality.
IV. Thus, by demonstrating how members of these groups feel about the two words, the study has proved to be useful for political analysts in several European countries.
V. According to the study, socialists and liberals rank both freedom and equality very high, while fascists rate both very low.
The CORRECT answer is:
A. III, V, I, II, IV
B. V, IV, III, I, II
C. III, V, IV, II, I
D. III, I, II, IV, V

6.____

7. I. "Can there be anything more amazing than this?"
    II. If the riddle is successfully answered, his dead brothers will be brought back to life.
    III. "Even though man sees those around him dying every day," says Dharmaraj, "he still believes and acts as if he were immortal."
    IV. "What is the cause of ceaseless wonder?" asks the Lord of the Lake.
    V. In the ancient epic, The Mahabharata, a riddle is asked of one of the Pandava brothers.
    The CORRECT answer is:
    A. V, II, I, IV, III
    B. V, IV, III, I, II
    C. V, II, IV, III, I
    D. V, II, IV, I, III

8. I. On the contrary, the two main theories—the cooperative (neoclassical) theory and the radical (labor theory)—clearly rest on very different assumptions, which have very different ethical overtones.
    II. The distribution of income is the primary factor in determining the relative levels of material well-being that different groups or individuals attain.
    III. Of all issues in economics, the distribution of income is one of the most controversial.
    IV. The neoclassical theory tends to support the existing income distribution (or minor changes), while the labor theory ends to support substantial changes in the way income is distributed.
    V. The intensity of the controversy reflects the fact that different economic theories are not purely neutral, *detached* theories with no ethical or moral implications.
    The CORRECT answer is:
    A. II, I, V, IV, III
    B. III, II, V, I, IV
    C. III, V, II, I, IV
    D. III, V, IV, I, II

9. I. The pool acts as a broker and ensures that the cheapest power gets used first.
    II. Every six seconds, the pool's computer monitors all of the generating stations in the state and decides which to ask for more power and which to cut back.
    III. The buying and selling of electrical power is handled by the New York Power Pool in Guilderland, New York.
    IV. This is to the advantage of both the buying and selling utilities.
    V. The pool began operation in 1970, and consists of the state's eight electric utilities.
    The CORRECT answer is:
    A. V, I, II, III, IV
    B. IV, II, I, III, V
    C. III, V, I, IV, II
    D. V, III, IV, II, I

10. I. Modern English is much simpler grammatically than Old English.
    II. Finnish grammar is very complicated; there are some fifteen cases, for example.
    III. Chinese, a very old language, may seem to be the exception, but it is the great number of characters/words that must be mastered that makes it so difficult to learn, not its grammar.
    IV. The newest literary language—that is, written as well as spoken—is Finish, whose literary roots go back only to about the middle of the nineteenth century.
    V. Contrary to popular belief, the longer a language is been in use the simpler its grammar—not the reverse.
    The CORRECT answer is:
    A. IV, I, II, III, V
    B. V, I, IV, II, III
    C. I, II, IV, III, V
    D. IV, II, III, I, V

KEY (CORRECT ANSWERS)

1.	D	6.	A
2.	A	7.	C
3.	C	8.	B
4.	D	9.	C
5.	C	10.	B

TEST 2

DIRECTIONS: This type of question tests your ability to recognize accurate paraphrasing, well-constructed paragraphs, and appropriate style and tone. It is important that the answer you select contains only the facts or concepts given in the original sentences. It is also important that you be aware of incomplete sentences, inappropriate transitions, unsupported opinions, incorrect usage, and illogical sentence order. Paragraphs that do not include all the necessary facts and concepts, that distort them, or that add new ones are not considered correct.

The format for this section may vary. Sometimes, long paragraphs are given, and emphasis is placed on style and organization. Our first five questions are of this type. Other times, the paragraphs are shorter, and there is less emphasis on style and more emphasis on accurate representation of information. Our second group of five questions are of this nature.

For each of Questions 1 through 10, select the paragraph that BEST expresses the ideas contained in the sentences above it. *PRINT THE LETTER OF THE CORRECT ANSWER IN THE SPACE AT THE RIGHT.*

1.   I. Listening skills are very important for managers.   1.____
   II. Listening skills are not usually emphasized.
   III. Whenever managers are depicted in books, manuals or the media, they are always talking, never listening.
   IV. We'd like you to read the enclosed handout on listening skills and to try to consciously apply them this week.
   V. We guarantee they will improve the quality of your interactions.

   A. Unfortunately, listening skills are not usually emphasized for managers. Managers are always depicted as talking, never listening. We'd like you to read the enclosed handout on listening skills. Please try to apply these principles this week. If you do, we guarantee they will improve the quality of your interactions.
   B. The enclosed handout on listening skills will be important improving the quality of your interactions. We guarantee it. All you have to do is take sometime this week to read and to consciously try to apply the principles. Listening skills are very important for manages, but they are not usually emphasized. Whenever managers are depicted in books, manuals or the media, they are always talking, never listening.
   C. Listening well is one of the most important skills a manager can have, yet it's not usually given much attention. Think about any representation of managers in books, manuals, or in the media that you may have seen. They're always talking, never listening. We'd like you to read the enclosed handout on listening skills and consciously try to apply them the rest of the week. We guarantee you will see a difference in the quality of your interactions.

2 (#2)

   D. Effective listening, one very important tool in the effective manager's arsenal, is usually not emphasized enough. The usual depiction of managers in books, manuals or the media is one in which they are always talking, never listening. We'd like you to read the enclosed handout and consciously try to apply the information contained therein throughout the rest of the week. We feel sure that you will see a marked difference in the quality of your interactions.

2. I. Chekhov wrote three dramatic masterpieces which share certain themes and formats: Uncle Vanya, The Cherry Orchard, and The Three Sisters.
   II. They are primarily concerned with the passage of time and how this erodes human aspirations.
   III. The plays are haunted by the ghosts of the wasted life.
   IV. The characters are concerned with life's lesser problems; however, such as the inability to make decisions, loyalty to the wrong cause, and the inability to be clear.
   V. This results in sweet, almost aching, type of a sadness referred to as Chekhovian.

2._____

   A. Chekhov wrote three dramatic masterpieces: Uncle Vanya, The Cherry Orchard, and The Three Sisters. These masterpieces share certain themes and formats: the passage of time, how time erodes human aspirations, and the ghosts of wasted life. Each masterpiece is characterized by a sweet, almost aching, type of sadness that has become known as Chekhovian. The sweetness of this sadness hinges on the fact that it is not the great tragedies of life which are destroying these characters, but their minor flaws: indecisiveness, misplaced loyalty, unclarity.
   B. The Cherry Orchard, Uncle Vanya, and The Three Sisters are three dramatic masterpieces written by Chekhov that use similar formats to explore a common theme. Each is primarily concerned with the way that passing time wears down human aspirations, and each is haunted by the ghosts of the wasted life. The characters are shown struggling futilely with the lesser problems of life: indecisiveness, loyalty to the wrong cause, and the inability to be clear. These struggles create a mood of sweet, almost aching, sadness that has become known as Chekhovian.
   C. Chekhov's dramatic masterpieces are, along with The Cherry Orchard, Uncle Vanya, and The Three Sisters. These plays share certain thematic and formal similarities. They are concerned most of all with the passage of time and the way in which time erodes human aspirations. Each play is haunted by the specter of the wasted life. Chekhov's characters are caught, however, by life's lesser snares: indecisiveness, loyalty to the wrong cause, and unclarity. The characteristic mood is a sweet, almost aching type of sadness that has come to be known as Chekhovian.
   D. A Chekhovian mood is characterized by sweet, almost aching, sadness. The term comes from three dramatic tragedies by Chekhov which revolve around the sadness of a wasted life. The three masterpieces (Uncle Vanya, The Three Sisters, and The Cherry Orchard) share the same

theme and format. The plays are concerned with how the passage of time erodes human aspirations. They are peopled with characters who are struggling with life's lesser problems. These are people who are indecisive, loyal to the wrong causes, or are unable to make themselves clear.

3. I. Movie previews have often helped producers decide which parts of movies they should take out or leave in.
    II. The first 1933 preview of King Kong was very helpful to the producers because many people ran screaming from the theater and would not return when four men first attacked by Kong were eaten by giant spiders.
    III. The 1950 premiere of Sunset Boulevard resulted in the filming of an entirely new beginning, and a delay of six months in the film's release.
    IV. In the original opening scene, William Holden was in a morgue talking with thirty-six other "corpses" about the ways some of them had died.
    V. When he began to tell them of his life with Gloria Swanson, the audience found this hilarious, instead of taking the scene seriously.

    A. Movie previews have often helped producers decide what parts of movies they should leave in or take out. For example, the first preview of King Kong in 1933 was very helpful. In one scene, four men were first attacked by Kong and then eaten by giant spiders. Many members of the audience ran screaming from the theater and would not return. The premiere of the 1950 film Sunset Boulevard was also very helpful. In the original opening scene, William Holden was in a morgue with thirty-six other "corpses," discussing the ways some of them had died. When he began to tell them of his life with Gloria Swanson, the audience found this hilarious. They were supposed to take the scene seriously. The result was a delay of six months in the release of the film while a new beginning was added.
    B. Movie previews have often helped producers decide whether they should change various parts of a movie. After the 1933 preview of King Kong, a scene in which four men who had been attacked by Kong were eaten by giant spiders was taken out as many people ran screaming from the theater and would not return. The 1950 premiere of Sunset Boulevard also led to some changes. In the original opening scene, William Holden was in a morgue talking with thirty-six other "corpses" about the ways some of them had died. When he began to tell them of his life with Gloria Swanson, the audience found this hilarious, instead of taking the scene seriously.
    C. What do Sunset Boulevard and King Kong have in common? Both show the value of using movie previews to test audience reaction. The first 1933 preview of King Kong showed that a scene showing four men being eaten by giant spiders after having been attacked by Kong was too frightening for many people. They ran screaming from the theater and couldn't be coaxed back. The 1950 premiere of Sunset Boulevard was also a scream, but not the kind the producers intended. The movie opens

3._____

with William Holden lying in a morgue discussing the ways they had died with thirty-six other "corpses." When he began to tell them of his life with Gloria Swanson, the audience couldn't take him seriously. Their laughter caused a six-month delay while the beginning was rewritten.

D. Producers very often use movie previews to decide if changes are needed. The premiere of Sunset Boulevard in 1950 led to a new beginning and a six-month delay in film release. At the beginning, William Holden and thirty-six other "corpses" discuss the ways some of them died. Rather than taking this seriously, the audience thought it was hilarious when he began to tell them of his life with Gloria Swanson. The first 1933 preview of King Kong was very helpful for its producers because one scene so terrified the audience that many of them ran screaming from the theater and would not return. In this particular scene, four men who had first been attacked by Kong were eaten by giant spiders.

4.
I. It is common for supervisors to view employees as "things" to be manipulated.
II. This approach does not motivate employees, nor does the carrot-and-stick approach because employees often recognize these behaviors and resent them.
III. Supervisors can change these behaviors by using self-inquiry and persistence.
IV. The best managers genuinely respect those they work with, are supportive and helpful, and are interested in working as a team with those they supervise.
V. They disagree with the Golden Rule that says "he or she who has the gold makes the rules."

4._____

A. Some managers act as if they think the Golden Rule means "he or she who has the gold makes the rules." They show disrespect to employees by seeing them as "things" to be manipulated. Obviously, this approach does not motivate employees any more than the carrot-and-stick approach motivates them. The employees are smart enough to spot these behaviors and resent them. On the other hand, the managers genuinely respect those they work with, are supportive and helpful, and are interested in working as a team. Self-inquiry and persistence can change even the former type of supervisor into the latter.

B. Many supervisors all into the trap of viewing employees as "things" to be manipulated, or try to motivate them by using a carrot-and-stick approach. These methods do not motivate employees, who often recognize the behaviors and resent them. Supervisors can change these behaviors, however, by using self-inquiry and persistence. The best managers are supportive and helpful, and have genuine respect for those with whom they work. They are interested in working as a team with those they supervise. To them, the Golden Rule is not "he or she who has the gold makes the rules."

C. Some supervisors see employees as "things" to be used or manipulated using a carrot-and-stick technique. These methods don't work. Employees often see through them and resent them. A supervisor who wants to change may do so. The techniques of self-inquiry and persistence can be used to turn him or her into the type of supervisor who doesn't think the Golden Rule is "he or she who has the gold makes the rules." They may become like the best managers who treat those with whom they work with respect and give them help and support. These are the manager who know how to build a team.

D. Unfortunately, many supervisors act as if their employees are objects whose movements they can position at will. This mistaken belief has the same result as another popular motivational technique—the carrot-and-stick approach. Both attitudes can lead to the same result—resentment from those employees who recognize the behaviors for what they are. Supervisors who recognize these behaviors can change through the use of persistence and the use of self-inquiry. It's important to remember that the best managers respect their employees. They readily give necessary help and support and are interested in working as a team with those they supervise. To these managers, the Golden Rule is not "he or she who has the gold makes the rules."

5.
I. The first half of the nineteenth century produced a group of pessimistic poets—Byron, De Musset, Heine, Pushkin, and Leopardi.
II. It also produced a group of pessimistic composers—Schubert, Chopin, Schumann, and even the later Beethoven.
III. Above all, in philosophy, there was the profoundly pessimistic philosopher, Schopenhauer.
IV. The Revolution was dead, the Bourbons were restored, the feudal barons were reclaiming their land, and progress everywhere was being suppressed, as the great age was over.
V. "I thank God," said Goethe, "that I am not young in so thoroughly finished a world."

5._____

A. "I thank God," said Goethe, "that I am not young in so thoroughly finished a world." The Revolution was dead, the Bourbons were restored, the feudal barons were reclaiming their land, and progress everywhere was being suppressed. The first half of the nineteenth century produced a group of pessimistic poets: Byron, De Musset, Heine, Pushkin, and Leopardi. It also produced pessimistic composers: Schubert, Chopin, Schumann. Although Beethoven came later, he fits into this group, too. Finally and above all, it also produced a profoundly pessimistic philosopher, Schopenhauer. The great age was over.

B. The first half of the nineteenth century produced a group of pessimistic poets: Byron, De Musset, Heine, Pushkin, and Leopardi. It produced a group of pessimistic composers: Schubert, Chopin, Schumann, and even the later Beethoven. Above all, it produced a profoundly pessimistic philosopher, Schopenhauer. For each of these men, the great age was over. The Revolution was dead, and the Bourbons were restored. The feudal barons were reclaiming their land, and progress everywhere was being suppressed.

C. The great age was over. The Revolution was dead—the Bourbons were restored, and the feudal barons were reclaiming their land. Progress everywhere was being suppressed. Out of this climate came a profound pessimism. Poets, like Byron, De Musset, Heine, Pushkin, and Leopardi; composers, like Schubert, Chopin, Schumann, and even the later Beethoven; and above all, a profoundly pessimistic philosopher, Schopenauer. This pessimism which arose in the first half of the nineteenth century is illustrated by these words of Goethe, "I thank God that I am not young in so thoroughly finished a world."

D. The first half of the nineteenth century produced a group of pessimistic poets, Byron, De Musset, Heine, Pushkin, and Leopardi—and a group of pessimistic composers, Schubert, Chopin, Schumann, and the later Beethoven. Above it all, it produced a profoundly pessimistic philosopher, Schopenhauer. The great age was over. The Revolution was dead, the Bourbons were restored, the feudal barons were reclaiming their land, and progress everywhere was being suppressed. "I thank God," said Goethe, "that I am not young in so thoroughly finished a world."

6. I. A new manager sometimes may feel insecure about his or her competence in the new position.
   II. The new manager may then exhibit defensive or arrogant behavior towards those one supervises, or the new manager may direct overly flattering behavior toward one's new supervisor.

   A. Sometimes, a new manager may feel insecure about his or her ability to perform well in this new position. The insecurity may lead him or her to treat others differently. He or she may display arrogant or defensive behavior towards those he or she supervises, or be overly flattering to his or her new supervisor.
   B. A new manager may sometimes feel insecure about his or her ability to perform well in the new position. He or she may then become arrogant, defensive, or overly flattering towards those he or she works with.
   C. There are times when a new manager may be insecure about how well he or she can perform in the new job. The new manager may also behave defensive or act in an arrogant way towards those he or she supervises, or overly flatter his or her boss.
   D. Sometimes a new manager may feel insecure about his or her ability to perform well in the new position. He or she may then display arrogant or defensive behavior towards those they supervise, or become overly flattering towards their supervisors.

6._____

7. I. It is possible to eliminate unwanted behavior by bringing it under stimulus control—tying the behavior to a cue, and then never, or rarely, giving the cue.
   II. One trainer successfully used this method to keep an energetic young porpoise from coming out of her tank whenever she felt like it, which was potentially dangerous.
   III. Her trainer taught her to do it for a reward, in response to a hand signal, and then rarely gave the signal.

7._____

A. Unwanted behavior can be eliminated by tying the behavior to a cue, and then never, or rarely, giving the cue. This is called stimulus control. One trainer was able to use this method to keep an energetic young porpoise from coming out of her tank by teaching her to come out for a reward in response to a hand signal, and then rarely giving the signal.
B. Stimulus control can be used to eliminate unwanted behavior. In this method, behavior is tied to a cue, and then the cue is rarely, if ever, given. One trainer was able to successfully use stimulus control to keep an energetic young porpoise from coming out of her tank whenever she felt like it—a potentially dangerous practice. She taught the porpoise to come out for a reward when she gave a hand signal, and then rarely gave the signal.
C. It is possible to eliminate behavior that is undesirable by bringing it under stimulus control by tying behavior to a signal, and then rarely giving the signal. One trainer successfully used this method to keep an energetic porpoise from coming out of her tank, a potentially dangerous situation. Her trainer taught the porpoise to do it for a reward, in response to a hand signal, and then would rarely give the signal.
D. By using stimulus control, it is possible to eliminate unwanted behavior by tying the behavior to a cue, and then rarely or never give the cue. One trainer was able to use this method to successfully stop a young porpoise from coming out of her tank whenever she felt like it. To curb this potentially dangerous practice, the porpoise was taught by the trainer to come out of the tank for a reward, in response to a hand signal, and then rarely given the signal.

8. I. There is a great deal of concern over the safety of commercial trucks, caused by their greatly increased role in serious accidents since federal deregulation in 1981.
   II. Recently, 60 percent of trucks in New York and Connecticut and 70 percent of trucks in Maryland randomly stopped by state troopers failed safety inspections.
   III. Sixteen states in the United States require no training at all for truck drivers.

   A. Since federal deregulation in 1981, there has been a great deal of concern over the safety of commercial trucks, and their greatly increased role in serious accidents. Recently, 60 percent of trucks in New York and Connecticut, and 70 percent of trucks in Maryland failed safety inspections. Sixteen states in the United States require no training at all for truck drivers.
   B. There is a great deal of concern over the safety of commercial trucks since federal deregulation in 1981. Their role in serious accidents has greatly increased. Recently, 60 percent of trucks randomly stopped in Connecticut and New York and 70 percent in Maryland failed safety inspections conducted by state troopers. Sixteen states in the United States provide no training at all for truck drivers.
   C. Commercial trucks have a greatly increased role in serious accidents since federal deregulation in 1981. This has led to a great deal of concern.

8.____

Recently, 70 percent of trucks in Maryland and 60 percent of trucks in New York and Connecticut failed inspection of those that were randomly stopped by state troopers. Sixteen states in the United States require no training for all truck drivers.

D. Since federal deregulation in 1981, the role that commercial trucks have played in serious accidents has greatly increased, and this has led to a great deal of concern. Recently, 60 percent of trucks in New York and Connecticut, and 70 percent of trucks in Maryland randomly stopped by state troopers failed safety inspections. Sixteen states in the U.S. don't require any training for truck drivers.

9.
I. No matter how much some people have, they still feel unsatisfied and want more, or want to keep what they have forever.
II. One recent television documentary showed several people flying from New York to Paris for a one-day shopping spree to buy platinum earrings, because they were bored.
III. In Brazil, some people were ordering coffins that cost a minimum of $45,000 and are equipping them with deluxe stereos, televisions, and other graveyard necessities.

9.____

A. Some people, despite having a great deal, still feel unsatisfied and want more, or think they can keep what they have forever. One recent documentary on television showed several people enroute from Paris to New York for a one day shopping spree to buy platinum earrings, because they were bored. Some people in Brazil are even ordering coffins equipped with such graveyard necessities as deluxe stereos and televisions. The price of the coffins start at $45,000.
B. No matter how much some people have, they may feel unsatisfied. This leads them to want more, or to want to keep what they have forever. Recently, a television documentary depicting several people flying from New York to Paris for a one day shopping spree to buy platinum earrings. They were bored. Some people in Brazil are ordering coffins that cost at least $45,000 and come equipped with deluxe televisions, stereos and other necessary graveyard items.
C. Some people will be dissatisfied no matter how much they have. They may want more, or they may want to keep what they have forever. One recent television documentary showed several people, motivated by boredom, jetting from New York to Paris for a one-day shopping spree to buy platinum earrings. In Brazil, some people are ordering coffins equipped with deluxe stereos, televisions and other graveyard necessities. The minimum price for these coffins—$45,000.
D. Some people are never satisfied. No matter how much they have they still want more, or think they can keep what they have forever. One television documentary recently showed several people flying from New York to Paris for the day to buy platinum earrings because they were bored. In Brazil, some people are ordering coffins that cost $45,000 and are equipped with deluxe stereos, televisions and other graveyard necessities.

10.
I. A television signal or video signal has three parts.
II. Its parts are the black-and-white portion, the color portion, and the synchronizing (sync) pulses, which keep the picture stable.
III. Each video source, whether it's a camera or a video-cassette recorder contains its own generator of these synchronizing pulses to accompany the picture that it's sending in order to keep it steady and straight.
IV. In order to produce a clean recording, a video-cassette recorder must "lock-up" to the sync pulses that are part of the video it is trying to record, and this effort may be very noticeable if the device does not have gunlock.

10.____

A. There are three parts to a television or video signal: the black-and-white part, the color part, and the synchronizing (sync) pulses, which keep the picture stable. Whether it's a video-cassette recorder or a camera, each video source contains its own pulse that synchronizes and generates the picture it's sending in order to keep it straight and steady. A video-cassette recorder must "lock up" to the sync pulses that are part of the video it's trying to record. If the device doesn't have gunlock, this effort must be very noticeable.
B. A video signal or television is comprised of three parts: the black-and-white portion, the color portion, and the sync (synchronizing) pulses, which keep the picture stable. Whether it's a camera or a video-cassette recorder, each video source contains its own generator of these synchronizing pulses. These accompany the picture that it's sending in order to keep it straight and steady. A video-cassette recorder must "lock up" to the sync pulses that are part of the video it is trying to record in order to produce a clean recording. This effort may be very noticeable if the device does not have gunlock.
C. There are three parts to a television or video signal: the color portion, the black-and-white portion, and the sync (synchronizing pulses). These keep the picture stable. Each video source, whether it's a video-cassette recorder or a camera, generates these synchronizing pulses accompanying the picture it's sending in order to keep it straight and steady. If a clean recording is to be produced, a video-cassette recorder must store the sync pulses that are part of the video it is trying to record. This effort may not be noticeable if the device does not have gunlock.
D. A television signal or video signal has three parts: the black-and-white portion, the color portion, and the synchronizing (sync) pulses. It's the sync pulses which keep the picture stable, which accompany it and keep it steady and straight. Whether it's a camera or a video-cassette recorder, each video source contains its own generator of these synchronizing pulses. To produce a clean recording, a video-cassette recorder must "lock up" to the sync pulses that are part of the video it is trying to record. If the device does not have gunlock, this effort may be very noticeable.

KEY (CORRECT ANSWERS)

1. C
2. B
3. A
4. B
5. D

6. A
7. B
8. D
9. C
10. D

PREPARING WRITTEN MATERIAL
EXAMINATION SECTION
TEST 1

DIRECTIONS: Each question or incomplete statement is followed by several suggested answers or completions. Select the one that BEST answers the question or completes the statement. *PRINT THE LETTER OF THE CORRECT ANSWER IN THE SPACE AT THE RIGHT.*

Questions 1-4.

DIRECTIONS: Questions 1 through 4 each consist of a sentence which may or may not be an example of good English. The underlined parts of each sentence may be correct or incorrect. Examine each sentence, considering grammar, punctuation, spelling, and capitalization. If the English usage in the underlined parts of the sentence given is better than any of the changes in the underlined words suggested in options B, C, or D, choose option A. If the changes in the underlined words suggested in options B, C, or D would make the sentence correct, choose the correct option. Do not choose an option that will change the meaning of the sentence.

1. This Fall, the office will be closed on Columbus Day, October 9th. 1.____
   A. Correct as is
   B. fall...Columbus Day; October
   C. Fall...columbus day, October
   D. fall...Columbus Day – October

2. There weren't no paper in the supply closet. 2.____
   A. Correct as is
   B. weren't any
   C. wasn't any
   D. wasn't no

3. The alphabet, or A to Z sequence are the basis of most filing systems. 3.____
   A. Correct as is
   B. alphabet, or A to Z sequence, is
   C. alphabet, or A to Z sequence, are
   D. alphabet, or A too Z sequence, is

4. The Office Aide checked the register and finding the date of the meeting. 4.____
   A. Correct as is
   B. regaster and finding
   C. register and found
   D. regaster and found

Questions 5-10.

DIRECTIONS: Questions 5 through 10 consist of sentences which contain examples of correct or incorrect English usage. Examine each sentence with reference to grammar, spelling, punctuation, and capitalization. Chooses one of the following options that would be BEST for correct English usage:

133

A. The sentence is correct
B. There is one mistake
C. There are two mistakes
D. There are three mistakes

5. Mrs. Fitzgerald came to the 59th Precinct to retreive her property which were stolen earlier in the week.

6. The two officer's responded to the call, only to find that the perpatrator and the victim have left the scene.

7. Mr. Coleman called the 61st Precinct to report that, upon arriving at his store, he discovered that there was a large hole in the wall and that three boxes of radios were missing.

8. The Administrative Leiutenant of the 62nd Precinct held a meeting which was attended by all the civilians, assigned to the Precinct.

9. Three days after the robbery occurred the detective apprahended two suspects and recovered the stolen items.

10. The Community Affairs Officer of the 64th Precinct is the liaison between the Precinct and the community; he works closely with various community organizations, and elected officials,

Questions 11-18.

DIRECTIONS: Questions 11 through 18 are to be answered on the basis of the following paragraph, which contains some deliberate errors in spelling and/or grammar and/or punctuation. Each line of the paragraph is preceded by a number. There are 9 lines and 9 numbers.

Line No.	Paragraph Line
1	The protection of life and proporty are, one of
2	the oldest and most important functions of a city.
3	New York City has it's own full-time police Agency.
4	The police Department has the power an it shall
5	be there duty to preserve the Public piece,
6	prevent crime detect and arrest offenders, supress
7	riots, protect the rites of persons and property, etc.
8	The maintainance of sound relations with the community they
9	serve is an important function of law enforcement officers

11. How many errors are contained in line one?

12. How many errors are contained in line two?

13. How many errors are contained in line three?

14. How many errors are contained in line four? 14._____

15. How many errors are contained in line five? 15._____

16. How many errors are contained in line six? 16._____

17. How many errors are contained in line seven? 17._____

18. How many errors are contained in line eight? 18._____

19. In the sentence, *The candidate wants to file his application for preference before it is too late*, the word *before* is used as a(n) 19._____
    A. preposition   B. subordinating conjunction
    C. pronoun   D. adverb

20. The one of the following sentences which is grammatically PREFERABLE to the others is: 20._____
    A. Our engineers will go over your blueprints so that you may have no problems in construction.
    B. For a long time he had been arguing that we, not he, are to blame for the confusion.
    C. I worked on this automobile for two hours and still cannot find out what is wrong with it.
    D. Accustomed to all kinds of hardships, fatigue seldom bothers veteran policemen.

KEY (CORRECT ANSWERS)

1.	A	11.	C
2.	C	12.	D
3.	B	13.	C
4.	C	14.	B
5.	C	15.	C
6.	D	16.	B
7.	A	17.	A
8.	C	18.	A
9.	C	19.	B
10.	B	20.	A

TEST 2

DIRECTIONS: Each question or incomplete statement is followed by several suggested answers or completions. Select the one that BEST answers the question or completes the statement. *PRINT THE LETTER OF THE CORRECT ANSWER IN THE SPACE AT THE RIGHT.*

1. The plural of 1.____
   A. turkey is turkies
   B. cargo is cargoes
   C. bankruptcy is bankruptcys
   D. son-in-law is son-in-laws

2. The abbreviation *viz.* means MOST NEARLY 2.____
   A. namely   B. for example   C. the following   D. see

3. In the sentence, *A man in a light-grey suit waited thirty-five minutes in the ante-room for the all-important document,* the word IMPROPERLY hyphenated is 3.____
   A. light-grey   B. thirty-five   C. ante-room   D. all-important

4. The MOST accurate of the following sentences is: 4.____
   A. The commissioner, as well as his deputy and various bureau heads, were present.
   B. A new organization of employers and employees have been formed.
   C. One or the other of these men have been selected.
   D. The number of pages in the book is enough to discourage a reader.

5. The MOST accurate of the following sentences is: 5.____
   A. Between you and me, I think he is the better man.
   B. He was believed to be me.
   C. Is it us that you wish to see?
   D. The winners are him and her.

Questions 6-13.

DIRECTIONS: The sentences numbered 6 through 13 deal with some phase of police activity. They may be classified most appropriately under one of the following four categories.

    A. Faulty because of incorrect grammar
    B. Faulty because of incorrect punctuation
    C. Faulty because of incorrect use of a word
    D. Correct

Examine each sentence carefully. Then, in the space at the right, print the capital letter preceding the option which is the BEST of the four suggested above. All incorrect sentences contain only one type of error. Consider a sentence correct if it contains none of the types of errors mentioned, even though there may be other correct ways of expressing the same thought.

2 (#2)

6. The Department Medal of Honor is awarded to a member of the Police Force who distinguishes himself inconspicuously in the line of police duty by the performance of an act of gallantry.

6._____

7. Members of the Detective Division are charged with the prevention of crime, the detection and arrest of criminals and the recovery of lost or stolen property,

7._____

8. Detectives are selected from the uniformed patrol forces after they have indicated by conduct, aptitude and performance that they are qualified for the more intricate duties of a detective.

8._____

9. The patrolman, pursuing his assailant, exchanged shots with the gunman and immortally wounded him as he fled into a nearby building.

9._____

10. The members of the Traffic Division has to enforce the Vehicle and Traffic Law, the Traffic Regulations and ordinances relating to vehicular and pedestrian traffic.

10._____

11. After firing a shot at the gunman, the crowd dispersed from the patrolman's line of fire.

11._____

12. The efficiency of the Missing Persons Bureau is maintained with a maximum of public personnel due to the specialized training given to its members.

12._____

13. Records of persons arrested for violations of Vehicle and Traffic Regulations are transmitted upon request to precincts, courts and other authorized agencies.

13._____

14. Following are two sentences which may or may not be written in correct English:
    I. Two clients assaulted the officer.
    II. The van is illegally parked.
   Which one of the following statements is CORRECT?
    A. Only Sentence I is written in correct English.
    B. Only Sentence II is written in correct English.
    C. Sentences I and II are both written in correct English.
    D. Neither Sentence I nor Sentence II is written in correct English.

14._____

15. Following are two sentences which may or may not be written in correct English:
    I. Security Officer Rollo escorted the visitor to the patrolroom.
    II. Two entry were made in the facility logbook.
   Which one of the following statements is CORRECT?
    A. Only Sentence I is written in correct English.
    B. Only Sentence II is written in correct English.
    C. Sentences I and II are both written in correct English.
    D. Neither Sentence I nor Sentence II is written in correct English.

15._____

16. Following are two sentences which may or may not be written in correct English:
    I. Officer McElroy putted out a small fire in the wastepaper basket.
    II. Special Officer Janssen told the visitor where he could obtained a pass.
    Which one of the following statements is CORRECT?
    A. Only Sentence I is written in correct English.
    B. Only Sentence II is written in correct English.
    C. Sentences I and II are both written in correct English.
    D. Neither Sentence I nor Sentence II is written in correct English.

    16.____

17. Following are two sentences which may or may not be written in correct English:
    I. Security Officer Warren observed a broken window while he was on his post in Hallway C.
    II. The worker reported that two typewriters had been stolen from the office,
    Which one of the following statements is CORRECT?
    A. Only Sentence I is written in correct English.
    B. Only Sentence II is written in correct English.
    C. Sentences I and II are both written in correct English.
    D. Neither Sentence I nor Sentence II is written in correct English,

    17.____

18. Following are two sentences which may or may not be written in correct English:
    I. Special Officer Cleveland was attempting to calm an emotionally disturbed visitor.
    II. The visitor did not stop crying and calling for his wife.
    Which one of the following statements is CORRECT?
    A. Only Sentence I is written in correct English.
    B. Only Sentence II is written in correct English.
    C. Sentences I and II are both written in correct English.
    D. Neither Sentence I nor Sentence II is written in correct English.

    18.____

19. Following are two sentences that may or may not be written in correct English:
    I. While on patrol, I observes a vagrant loitering near the drug dispensary.
    II. I escorted the vagrant out of the building and off the premises.
    Which one of the following statements is CORRECT?
    A. Only Sentence I is written in correct English.
    B. Only Sentence II is written in correct English.
    C. Sentences I and II are both written in correct English.
    D. Neither Sentence I nor Sentence II is written in correct English.

    19.____

20. Following are two sentences which may or may not be written in correct English:
    I. At 4:00 P.M., Sergeant Raymond told me to evacuate the waiting area immediately due to a bomb threat.
    II. Some of the clients did not want to leave the building.
    Which one of the following statements is CORRECT?
    A. Only Sentence I is written in correct English.
    B. Only Sentence II is written in correct English.
    C. Sentences I and II are both written in correct English.
    D. Neither Sentence I nor Sentence II is written in correct English.

    20.____

KEY (CORRECT ANSWERS)

1.	B	11.	A
2.	A	12.	C
3.	C	13.	D
4.	D	14.	C
5.	A	15.	A
6.	C	16.	D
7.	B	17.	A
8.	D	18.	A
9.	C	19.	B
10.	A	20.	C

COMMON DIAGNOSTIC NORMS

CONTENTS

		Page
1.	Respiration	1
2.	Pulse-Rate	1
3.	Blood Pressure	1
4.	Blood Metabolism	1
5.	Blood	1
6.	Urine	3
7.	Spinal Fluid	4
8.	Snellen Chart Fractions	4

COMMON DIAGNOSTIC NORMS

1. RESPIRATION: From 16-20 per minute.

2. PULSE-RATE: Men, about 72 per minute.
   Women, about 80 per minute.

3. BLOOD PRESSURE:
   Men: 110-135 (Systolic)   Women: 95-125   (Systolic)
        70-85   (Diastolic)   65-70   (Diastolic)

4. BASAL METABOLISM: Represents the body energy expended to maintain respiration, circulation, etc. Normal rate ranges from plus 10 to minus 10.

5. BLOOD:

   a. Red Blood (Erythrocyte) Count:
   Male adult - 5,000,000 per cu. mm.
   Female adult - 4,500,000 per cu. mm.
   (Increased in polycythemia vera, poisoning by carbon monoxide, in chronic pulmonary artery sclerosis, and in concentration of blood by sweating, vomiting, or diarrhea.)
   (Decreased in pernicious anemia, secondary anemia, and hypochronic anemia.)
   b. White Blood (Leukocyte) Count: 6,000 to 8,000 per cu. mm.
   (Increased with muscular exercise, acute infections, intestinal obstruction, coronary thrombosis, leukemias.)
   (Decreased due to injury to source of blood formation and interference in delivery of cells to bloodstream, typhoid, pernicious anemia, arsenic and benzol poisoning.)
   The total leukocyte group is made up of a number of diverse varieties of white blood cells. Not only the total leukocyte count, but also the relative count of the diverse varieties, is an important aid to diagnosis. In normal blood, from:
   70-72% of the leukocytes are *polymorphonuclear neuirophils.*
   2-4% of the leukocytes are *polymorphonuclear eosinophils.*
   0-.5% of the leukocytes are *basophils,*
   20-25% of the leukocytes are *lymphocytes.*
   2-6% of the leukocytes are *monocytes.*
   c. Blood Platelet (Thrombocyte) Count:
   250,000 per cu. mm. Blood platelets are important in blood coagulation.

   d. Hemoglobin Content:
   May normally vary from 85-100%. A 100% hemoglobin content is equivalent to the presence of 15.6 grams of hemoglobin in 100 c.c. of blood.
   e. Color Index:
   Represents the relative amount of hemoglobin contained in a red blood corpuscle compared with that of a normal individual of the patient's age and sex.
   The normal is 1. To determine the color index, the percentage of hemoglobin is divided by the ratio of red cells in the patient's blood to a norm of 5,000,000. Thus, a hemoglobin content of 60% and a red cell count of 4,000,000 (80% of 5,000,000) produces an abnormal color index of .75.

f. Sedimentation Rate:
Represents the measurement of the speed with which red cells settle toward the bottom of a containing vessel. The rate is expressed in millimeters per hour, and indicates the total sedimentation of red blood cells at the end of 60 minutes.

Average rate:	4-7 mm. in 1 hour
Slightly abnormal rate:	8-15 mm. in 1 hour
Moderately abnormal rate:	16-40 mm. in 1 hour
Considerably abnormal rate:	41-80 mm. in 1 hour

(The sedimentation rate is above normal in patients with chronic infections, or in whom there is a disease process involving destruction of tissue, such as coronary thrombosis, etc.)

g. Blood Sugar:
90-120 mg. per 100 c.c. (Normal)
In mild diabetics: 150-300 mg. per 100 c.c.
In severe diabetics: 300-1200 mg. per 100 c.c.

h. Blood Lead:
0.1 mg. or less in 100 c.c. (Normal). Greatly increased in lead poisoning.

i. Non-Protein Nitrogen:
Since the function of the kidneys is to remove from the blood certain of the waste products of cellular activity, any degree of accumulation of these waste products in the blood is a measure of renal malfunction. For testing purposes, the substances chosen for measurement are the nitrogen-containing products of protein combustion, their amounts being estimated in terms of the nitrogen they contain. These substances are urea, uric acid, and creatinine, the sum total of which, in addition to any traces of other waste products, being designated as total non-protein nitrogen (NPN).

The normal limits of NPN in 100 c.c. of blood range from 25-40 mg. Of this total, urea nitrogen normally constitutes 12-15 mg., uric acid 2-4 mg., and creatinine 1-2 mg.

6. URINE:

a. Urine - Lead:
0.08 mg. per liter of urine (normal).
(Increased in lead poisoning.)

b. Sugar:
From none to a faint trace (normal).
From 0.5% upwards (abnormal).
(Increased in diabetes mellitus.)

c. Urea:
Normal excretion ranges from 15-40 grams in 24 hours.
(Increased in fever and toxic states.)

d. Uric Acid:
Normal excretion is variable. (Increased in leukemia and gout.)

e. Albumin:
Normal renal cells allow a trace of albumin to pass into the urine, but this trace is so minute that it cannot be detected by ordinary tests.

f. Casts:
   In some abnormal conditions, the kidney tubules become lined with substances which harden and form a mould or *oast* inside the tubes. These are later washed out by the urine, and may be detected microscopically. They are named either from the substance composing them, or from their appearance. Thus, there are pus casts, epithelial casts from the walls of the tubes, hyaline casts formed from coagulable elements of the blood, etc.
g. Pus Cells:
   These are found in the urine in cases of nephritis or other inflammatory conditions of the urinary tract.
h. Epithelial Cells:
   These are always present in the urine. Their number is greatly multiplied, however, in inflammatory conditions of the urinary tract.
i. Specific Gravity:
   This is the ratio between the weight of a given volume of urine to that of the same volume of water. A normal reading ranges from 1.015 to 1.025. A high specific gravity usually occurs in diabetes mellitus. A low specific gravity is associated with a polyuria.

7. SPINAL FLUID:

   a. Spinal Fluid Pressure (Manometric Reading):
      100-200 mm. of water or 7-15 mm, of mercury (normal).
      (Increased in cerebral edema, cerebral hemorrhage, meningitis, certain brain tumors, or if there is some process blocking the fluid circulation in the spinal column, such as a tumor or herniated nucleus pulposus impinging on the spinal canal.)
   b. Quickenstedt's Sign:
      When the veins in the neck are compressed on one or both sides, there is a rapid rise in the pressure of the cerebrospinal fluid of healthy persons, and this rise quickly disappears when pressure is removed from the neck. But when there is a block of the vertebral canal, the pressure of the cerebrospinal fluid is little or not at all affected by this maneuver.
   c. Cerebrospinal Sugar:
      50-60 mg. per 100 c.c. of spinal fluid (normal).
      (Increased in epidemic encephalitis, diabetes mellitus, and increased intracranial pressure.)
      (Decreased in purulent and tuberculous meningitis.)
   d. Cerebrospinal Protein:
      15-40 mg. per 100 c.c. of spinal fluid (normal).
      (Increased in suppurative meningitis, epileptic seizures, cerebrospinal syphilis, anterior poliomyelitis, brain abscess, and brain tumor.)
   e. Colloidal Gold Test:
      This test is made to determine the presence of cerebrospinal protein.
   f. Cerebrospinal Cell Count:
      0-10 lymphocytes per cu. mm. (normal).
   g. Cerebrospinal Globulin:
      Normally negative. It is positive in various types of meningitis, various types of syphilis of the central nervous system, in poliomyelitis, in brain tumor, and in intracranial hemorrhage.

8. **SNELLEN CHART FRACTIONS AS SCHEDULE LOSS DETERMINANTS:**

   a. Visual acuity is expressed by a Snell Fraction, where the numerator represents the distance, in feet, between the subject and the test chart, and the denominator represents the distance, in feet, at which a normal eye could read a type size which the abnormal eye can read only at 20 feet.
   b. Thus, 20/20 means that an individual placed 20 feet from the test chart clearly sees the size of type that one with normal vision should see at that distance.
   c. 20/60 means that an individual placed 20 feet from the test chart can read only a type size, at a distance of 20 feet, which one of normal vision could read at 60 feet.
   d. Reduction of a Snellen Fraction to its simplest form roughly indicates the amount of vision remaining in an eye. Thus, a visual acuity of 20/60 corrected implies a useful vision of 1/3 or 33 1/3%, and a visual loss of 2/3 or 66 2/3% of the eye.

   Similarly:

Visual Acuity (Corrected)	Percentage Loss of Use of Eye
20/20	No loss
20/25	20%
20/30	33 1/3%
20/40	50%
20/50	60%
20/60	66 2/3%
20/70	70% (app.)
20/80	75%
20/100	100% (since loss of 80% or more constitutes industrial blindness)

www.ingramcontent.com/pod-product-compliance
Lightning Source LLC
Chambersburg PA
CBHW082149300426
44117CB00016B/2665